For Mom and Dad—
Always the wind beneath my wings

ଔ

To Lou and Deb—
"Love you more."

Acclaim for *Hurting in the Church*

"*Hurting in the Church* provides a psychologically wise and spiritually profound path forward for Catholics who have been abused, traumatized, or wounded by other Catholics—especially those in leadership. Father Berg writes out of his own and others' personal experiences of finding surprising and powerful grace and healing in the darkest of places. Chapter ten, on how to recover one's belief in and love for the Church, is worth the price of the book alone!"—**Sherry Weddell, best-selling author of** *Forming Intentional Disciples*

"An honest and much-needed book that addresses one of the most important problems in the Catholic Church today: the many Catholics who feel marginalized, ignored, hurt, insulted, and even abused by the Church. In his new book, Father Berg, who shares his own painful experiences with the Church, offers moving stories, helpful perspectives and healthy ways forward."—**Father James Martin, SJ, author of** *Jesus: A Pilgrimage*

"Father Berg ... writes with astonishing candor about his experience of hurting in the Church and how it brought him to seek to help others who have suffered from the sins of the members of the Mystical Body. *Hurting in the Church* is poised to become one of the most important works of pastoral theology of the twenty-first century. It is a must-read for Catholics as it shows us how to live up to our identity as a Church that goes out proactively to bring Christ's healing to those who are wounded—and first among them are those whom we ourselves have harmed."—**Dawn Eden Goldstein, STD, author of** *Remembering God's Mercy: Redeem the Past and Free Yourself from Painful Memories*

"Here is an unflinching examination of the Church's brokenness—from insensitive bureaucracy to the deep scars of sexual abuse—along with practical advice and the promise of hope for the challenging path forward. Fearless in his assessment, Father Berg is equally confident that in Jesus and with the help of the Holy Spirit we can move toward healing and wholeness. This is essential reading for a hurting Church." —**Cardinal Timothy Dolan, archbishop of New York**

"It took courage for Father Berg to write with such honesty and transparency, including about his personal hurts. And his courage will give you courage—the courage to not only confront the facts of sin and weakness within the Church, but also the courage to give God another chance to allow you to discover him once again within the embrace of Mother Church, despite the failings of her members."—**Father Jonathan Morris, author of** *The New York Times* **bestseller** *The Way of Serenity*

"Father Berg offers honest, hopeful, and prophetic insight into the deep pain of past hurts that many in the Church have experienced. The testimonies of real members of the wounded Body of Christ and the pain they have experienced is a loving clarion call to the whole Church to embrace a new revolution—a 'revolution of tenderness'—as a balm for those that have been hurt."—**Deacon Larry Oney, president, Hope & Purpose Ministries**

"In pages that are raw, honest, vulnerable—and at times provocative— Father Berg draws back the curtains on a world of hurt experienced by many Catholics. But naming the pain is not the end of the story. The surrender of memories, the struggle to forgive, the turn toward faith, the rediscovery of God's powerful love, and the gift of amazing peace—these are the milestones on our journey toward healing, toward deep intimacy with Jesus Christ. Father Berg is a wise and compassionate guide, the kind of priest each of us, in our most difficult moments, longs to find. And so, this book is a must-read for all Catholics, not only because we all need healing, but also because we all need help to help others heal."—**Mary Rice Hasson, director, Catholic Women's Forum, Ethics and Public Policy Center**

"Here is a compelling, refreshingly clear, and honest exposition of our need to enter the healing rays of Christ's own love. Born of the author's own pain and suffering, and brought to maturity by the integration of this pain into the mercy of the Christ, Father Berg has given the Church a bracing narrative, leaving the reader and all ecclesial ministers with a resource to lead the Church into a new freedom. This book, which carries ideas saturated in prayer, will itself become a vessel of healing for a Church that humbly seeks to renew itself in the Lord."—**Deacon James Keating, PhD, director of theological formation, Creighton University**

"Father Thomas Berg shares the medicine he discovered, and himself took to heal, giving the rest of us hope for the treatment of our own wounds and the wounds of others. He leads us on the path toward the Divine Physician and to the profound Christian catharsis that occurs when we purify our wounds through the redeeming blood that flowed from the wounded good Samaritan."—**Father Roger Landry, national chaplain, Catholic Voices USA**

HURTING
IN THE
CHURCH

A Way Forward
for Wounded Catholics

Father Thomas Berg

Our Sunday Visitor

www.osv.com
Our Sunday Visitor Publishing Division
Our Sunday Visitor, Inc.
Huntington, Indiana 46750

Nihil Obstat
Msgr. Michael Curran
Censor Deputatus

Imprimatur
✠ His Eminence, Timothy Michael Cardinal Dolan
Archbishop of New York
October 14, 2016

The *Nihil Obstat* and *Imprimatur* are official declarations that a book is free from doctrinal or moral error. It is not implied that those who have granted the *Nihil Obstat* and *Imprimatur* agree with the contents, opinions, or statements expressed.

CONTENTS

☙

Life is not about
Waiting for the storms to pass,
But about
*Learning to dance
In the rain.*

—Unknown

AUTHOR'S NOTE

CR

Even if you don't identify with the target audience I describe in the introduction, I hope that my book can still be worthwhile for you.

You don't have to be Catholic to benefit from this book. While I particularly have in mind the situation of baptized Catholics in the United States, I believe Catholics from around the globe as well as members of non-Catholic Christian denominations and faith communities will be able to benefit from the reflections and stories contained in the pages that follow.

You don't have to be a practicing Catholic to benefit from this book. In fact, I wrote much of it with the non-practicing Catholics in mind. So give it a shot: there's nothing to lose.

Or the hurts you are experiencing in life might not be faith-related at all. You might even be experiencing physical pain or long-term illness or emotional suffering that has another source. It's enough that you are carrying around wounds to benefit from these pages, especially chapters 6 through 9 which deal with personal healing.

But you don't have to be hurting at all to benefit from this book. Perhaps you know someone who is hurting; this book might give you some better insight into that person's situation and help you to love them better.

And let me offer a few quick thoughts on how to read this book. Obviously there is a certain logic to the order of the chapters and the progression of the book, but you shouldn't feel locked into reading the chapters in order. The chapters are generally independent of one another; so if a title or topic of a particular chapter grabs your attention, feel free to jump right in and read that chapter.

In most of the chapters, you will come across endnote references. Don't let them distract you. They just point to more information (found in the back of the book) that you can always return to and read later if you are interested. I've also included a list of some recommended reading that might afford you additional food for heart, mind, and soul.

Whoever you are and whatever your situation in life, know that I am praying for you—and asking God to touch your heart and bring you his peace through these pages.

INTRODUCTION

CR

A Church of the Hurting

This book has a very particular, though not exclusive, audience. I am writing for Catholics who, somewhere along life's journey, have had a painful experience in the Church.

To suggest that a large segment of the Catholic population, including those who no longer practice, fits this description might seem an exaggeration to some. What I am proposing could appear downright suspect or at least foreign to the experience of many readers. I would wager, however, that for many other readers, this book will strike a profound, if unsettling, chord.

The reality of the Catholic Church today in developed countries, and certainly in the United States, is that we are a church of the hurting. This book is for Catholics—far more than we would care to imagine—who have endured an experience of hurt in the Church. It is an exposé of our frequent failures as Catholics to live the life of genuine Christlike charity, the self-giving, passionate, interpersonal love and caring—*agapē*—experienced so intensely in the first Christian communities and envisioned by St. Paul in his first letter to the Corinthians, chapter 13. My book attempts to shed a spotlight on our decades-old tolerance of an unchristian status quo, what in many sectors—in our parishes, rectories, chanceries, and Catholic ministries—can at times degenerate into a veritable culture of hurt. I offer this book as an examination of conscience following the Year of Mercy, as an invitation to reflect on those areas where we are sorely lacking in charity in our faith communities, an invitation to an essential conversion of heart, and to a renewal of the life of charity in our local churches.

CR

Most of all, I offer this book as a source of solace, hope, and healing for wounded and struggling Catholics. Our pews are filled with them, while many have also gone missing: Catholics who have been subjected at one time or another in their experience of the Church to hurts of all shapes and sizes. Some—a percentage far larger, I suspect, than what most Catholics might imagine—have even suffered what can only be described as a *life-altering* harm in and through their experience of the Church. We are a Church that all too often, all too freely, all too callously and without regard, inflicts emotional wounds on its own.

Is it 1 in 5, or 1 in 10, or 1 in 300 Catholics who have had a painful experience in the Church, in their journey of faith? I am unaware of any surveys taken on the matter. But let's consider, for example, that the U.S. bishops have received to date more than 17,000 claims of sexual abuse by priests alleged to have occurred in the past several decades. Most experts would affirm that the actual number of victims of clergy sexual abuse in the United States—including those who have never come forward—could be ten times that number.

Sexual abuse constitutes a singular, maximal, and grotesque form of hurt. And yet—in our parishes, rectories, chanceries, and ministries—an honest examination of our ordinary experience as members of the Church in the United States confirms that on a daily basis we submit each other, by the hundreds, to other forms of hurt: impatience, angry outbursts, intolerance, denigration, manipulation, prejudice, abrasiveness, harassment, humiliation, intrigue, gossip, dishonesty, deception, detraction, calumny, betrayal—and the list could go on.

Some readers might characterize my claim as wildly exaggerated; others will say I have understated my case.

How do I support my contentions here?

I can only appeal to experience: I know too many hurting Catholics. And I will leave it to you, the reader, to judge whether my claim is wildly off the mark, or all too painfully true.

ଚ୍ଚ

One of the difficulties in writing a book like this is that in contemporary American culture, and consequently within the Church, the notions of "hurt" or "woundedness" are sometimes exaggerated. No doubt, it is easy these days to "play the hurt card."

That notwithstanding, today we have no other choice than *to take it very seriously when a brother or sister in Christ claims to have been hurt* in their experience of the Catholic Church. Genuine, Christlike love demands this of us. As founder of the Catholics Returning Home program, Sally Mews observes:

> Most people who have left the Church have a "church story" within which lies a big bundle of hurts. They may cite a reason for leaving which isn't the real or "root" cause. For example, some will say they have disagreements with some of the Church's theological positions, but after further discussion, they'll say they tried to arrange a wedding or funeral and the parish staff was unfriendly or uncooperative. Whatever the real reason for their leaving the Church, perception is reality.[1]

Perception is, indeed, reality when it comes to someone who is hurting. Hurt is very much in the eye of the beholder, in the subjective and very intimate personal experience of the one who has been on the receiving end of an emotionally painful experience.

Not to be overlooked, by the way, is that, grammatically, "to hurt" can be used both transitively and intransitively; it can mean to cause pain, as well as to experience pain. My reflections here, as it turns out, cut both ways. When we suffer in the Church, because of the Church, we are on the receiving end; there is a member of the Church who causes that hurt, who hurts *us*. The obvious upshot, of course, is that we are sometimes not on the receiving end; rather, we ourselves, as members of the Church, can also *do* the hurting. I write with the acute awareness that *I too have hurt brothers and sisters in the Church.*

ଓଃ

Riding the momentum of the Year of Mercy, I offer these reflections as a necessary examination of conscience, and a clarion call to Catholics to become healers of that sickly inner culture of our Church, so anemic in its capacity to love with genuine, Christlike love. We can contribute to this necessary transformation, purification, and renewal of the Church by praying for a robust influx of the supernatural virtue of charity in our lives and in our faith communities, and by committing ourselves to collaborate with that grace in new, intentional, and dynamic ways in our everyday lives.

That examination of conscience requires us to confront with honesty the reality that we are a Church of the hurting—in myriad ways. This is a truth which comes home to me every time I stand at the pulpit in church to preach: I look out on the faces staring back at me, and I *know* I am speaking to hurting individuals. We hurt first and foremost because *life hurts*: hurting is part of the human condition. And most would agree that mental and emotional pain is often much more challenging than the physical pain occasioned by serious illness or disability. When pain experienced in and through the Church is layered on to what life itself already deals us, the suffering can be all the more acute.

ଓଃ

The hurts I have in mind might have been suffered at the hands of a priest, deacon, educator, fellow parishioner, or bishop. I have in mind especially those who, like me, have suffered the deeper, devastating kind of hurt occasioned by the betrayal of trust. The hurts are manifold and can come in varying degrees of intensity:

- You were chewed out by a priest once when you were an altar server.

- You were horribly embarrassed by a priest's harsh reaction to something you said in confession, and you've never stepped inside a Catholic church since.

- You were abruptly let go from the Catholic grade school where you taught for many years—in a manner you found cold, spiteful, ungrateful, and degrading.

- You are a priest who feels emotionally exhausted from continually having to face the criticism, gossip, backbiting, and mean-spiritedness of a group of parishioners who simply do not like you.

- You were just received into the Catholic Church at Easter but are now dismayed by the lack of fellowship and indifference of your new "parish family."

- You feel heartbroken because a priest you loved and idealized for years was shown to be living a double-life of sexual and financial misconduct.

- You've turned utterly cynical about the Church because of the scandal of clergy sexual abuse.

- You are a priest suffering the public humiliation of being removed from ministry while under investigation for what you know to be a false accusation of sexual misconduct after decades of faithful and selfless ministry.

- You are a Catholic nun engaged in ministry to the elderly and homebound, and no one ever seems to notice your dedication, let alone thank you for your service.

- You are a Latino Catholic who feels treated like a second-class citizen at your predominantly white suburban parish.

- You experience same-sex attraction and feel conflicted about the Church's teaching on homosexuality.

- You are a priest who has developed a drinking problem, and you loathe yourself for it and are considering walking away from your ministry.

- You are a woman who has experienced a Church seemingly dominated by male clericalism.

- You are an elderly Catholic widow who never receives a visit from any parishioners, much less from your own parish priests.

- You are a bishop who feels you have no strength left to continue under the weight of loneliness and emotionally draining responsibilities.

- You were sexually abused by a member of the clergy as a child.

The wounds could be relatively superficial; the wounds might be deep and overwhelming. Some wounds heal quickly; others take a lifetime. And in our hearts we ask: Why does this happen? Why does it have to be this way?

ᏇᏗ

The word "scandal" comes from the Latin *scandalum*, meaning a stumbling block, obstacle, or trap. In the Vulgate Latin version of Matthew 16:23, when Jesus rebukes Peter, saying, "Get behind me, Satan," he adds, "you are to me a *scandalum*"—a stumbling block. The hurt inflicted upon us in our experience of the Church can be a stumbling block that trips us up, beats us down, knocks the wind out of us, disorients us, and can even shipwreck our Christian faith.

I have written this book because I, too, have been hurt in the Church. I've struggled with the agonizing bewilderment and the emotional and spiritual pain that can threaten to upend a journey of faith, rock our spiritual edifice to its very foundations, and bring us to the brink of spiritual collapse—even leading us to the unthinkable: to walk away from the Church and even to abandon the Christian faith altogether. And I have accompanied many of my brothers and sisters in the Faith through such experiences.

In reality, it doesn't take much for even a small hurt to become a major stumbling block to someone's Catholic faith. At the core of any degree of hurt occasioned in the Church is a kind of profound indignation—the gnawing sense that "this should not be happening!"

Our failures in love also cause scandal outside the Church. If the Church has ever succeeded in her mission, it was every time she was able—in the lives of faithful and committed Christians— to embody the self-sacrificing love exemplified by her Divine Spouse. What has always confounded her mission and identity— to the scorn and derision of non-Catholics—are the times her members have failed in that great task, the times we have failed to correspond to the mandate of our Savior: "Love one another as I have loved you." At the heart of our unholiness and brokenness, we discover our all-too-frequent failures to respond to the world and to each other with radical Christlike love.

☓

Is there hope for wounded Catholics? Certainly—and *that* ultimately is what this book is about. For Catholics who may have already walked away from the Church, this book is an invitation to reconsider. It's also meant for Catholics who, because of a powerfully negative experience, find themselves on the brink of walking away or of losing their faith, or who find their struggles to make progress in the faith very difficult. It's a book for those whose daily bread is doubt about the Church, recurring bitterness and inability to forgive, numbness and distaste for things spiritual, the loss of joy, tedium in slogging on in a ministry that now seems meaningless, the loss of affection for the Church.

For them and for anyone else who hurts in the Church or knows someone who hurts, I hope my book can serve to forge a way ahead and a way beyond the pain, to help readers understand—as I had to come to understand—that it is possible, in Christ and with the grace flowing from his Heart, to discover all of our hurts as a wellspring of graced living, and as a source of holiness and wholeness.

Part I explores in greater depth, although not exhaustively, some of the myriad ways we hurt in the Church today, beginning with my own personal story and weaving in the stories of others. It explores as well one of the most heinous forms of hurt—clerical sexual abuse—while also addressing the unique sufferings of priests, as well as the sufferings of those who feel alienated from the Church by her teachings, particularly those dealing with marriage and sexual morality.

Part II aims at offering wounded Catholics several avenues by which they cannot only enter more fully into a process of healing, but also discover anew the radiant and untarnished beauty of that same Church in which they have been so deeply hurt, and in which they can become—precisely because of the hurt they have endured—better human beings, and more committed and loving followers of Jesus Christ.

Part III turns our attention from our individual wounds to the wounds of the Mystical Body of Christ, the Church. Inspired by the teaching of Pope Francis, and still in the afterglow of the Year of Mercy, the final chapters invite us to a collective examination of conscience as to our living of radical, Christlike charity, and suggest some key actions and commitments that are essential in order to heal a hurting Church.

Part I
The Ways We Hurt

CHAPTER 1

◌જ

My Story

"She had the feeling that somehow, in the very far-off places, perhaps even in far-off ages, there would be a meaning found to all sorrow and an answer too fair and wonderful to be as yet understood."

— Hannah Hurnard, *Hinds' Feet on High Places*

So, why did I start writing this book?

Let's back up a ways.

I reached young adulthood in the mid-1980s. As a freshman at Marquette University in 1983, I had an experience—I called it a "conversion" at the time—that led me to a more lucid and deliberate commitment to my Catholic faith. These were still the years of considerable pastoral and liturgical upheaval following the Second Vatican Council. Now in college, I had emerged from that upheaval not only with my Catholic faith intact, but intensified by a newfound zeal. I had great hopes for the future of the Church and for my life in it. As time went on, it became clear that those hopes were anchored in a particular way in the person of Pope—now a saint—John Paul II, and in the Church's renewal movements.

Indeed, the experience in the United States and elsewhere, from the late seventies into the eighties, was that the Church was precisely in a time of renewal, a reality seemingly captured in the multiplicity of renewal movements across the globe, from Renew International (born as a program for parish-based Catholic spiritual renewal in Newark, New Jersey, in 1976) to Catholic charismatic renewal and many more. "Renewal" was the spiritual buzz-word of the 1980s.

This momentum took on an added dimension of urgency and excitement as a dominant theme began to emerge in the thought of Pope St. John Paul II: that we were actually protagonists in a great, new, noble, and holy endeavor, the "New Evangelization." The pope used the phrase for the first time in a significant and public manner on March 9, 1983, in Port-au-Prince, Haiti, in his opening address to the general assembly of the Latin American Episcopal Conference (CELAM).

In that speech, John Paul directed the bishops' attention to the upcoming fifth centennial of evangelization of the New World to be commemorated in 1992. That coming commemoration would attain to its full meaning, asserted the pontiff, only if the bishops, along with the clergy and lay faithful, were to embrace that anniversary with a renewed commitment, not to a project of re-evangelization, "but to a New Evangelization, new in its ardor, methods and expression."

By 1986, I was fully committed to that project and convinced that—just as Jesus wanted me to be—I was on the road to becoming a real player in this effort: I had joined a new religious community, the Legionaries of Christ, whose entire ethos was seemingly to bring about in the Church a new day of faith, a new evangelization, with new and more effective methods, to provoke and spearhead a renewal of the Catholic priesthood, to forge new inroads in apostolic efficacy—in a word, the Legionaries were going to play a decisive role in ushering in an era of vitality, youth, energy, action, and "results" in the Church.

I was twenty-one. I had discerned a vocation to the priesthood. I wanted to fully abandon myself to Jesus Christ and his Church. And in my mind, I could not be better positioned to do just that, and to make a lasting contribution to this great project—the New Evangelization—than as a member of the Legionaries.

CR

Those convictions about my religious community, and about my life within that community, began to be challenged eleven years later. In February 1997, nine former Legionaries of Christ went public with allegations of sexual abuse against the Legion's founder, Marcial Maciel Degollado.

I was studying in Rome at the time, not yet ordained a priest. To most of us within the congregation, this news was a bombshell. Yet we were somewhat shielded from the impact since we were not allowed, under obedience, to read the story itself (which had been published in the *Hartford Courant*). We were forbidden to seek out information from anyone outside of the congregation and discouraged from speaking about the matter even with our own superiors. And we were certainly not to discuss it among ourselves.

I, along with a few others, had access at the time to the newly emerging internet, but our access was controlled by a gatekeeping mechanism that required users to obtain permission for every site they wanted to visit. Under obedience, our superiors required us to forgo reading such articles and information that might otherwise come into our hands—a limited possibility anyway since our mail was screened and newspapers were edited before being left in the reading rooms. Anything deemed inappropriate (on any matter, not just news of Maciel) was clipped out by the superior.

Like any and all negative things that were ever publicly expressed about the Legion and could get to our ears, this bombshell, too, was quickly diffused and channeled into a void of internal congregational silence.

We knew the drill. If you considered yourself a faithful member of the congregation, you would strive internally to set aside any curiosity on the matter. Besides, throughout our years of formation, we had absorbed the congregation's narrative according to which, "enemies" of the Legion had time and time again plotted against Maciel, attempting to oppose "God's plan" for the congregation. Time and time again, those attempts were thwarted by "divine providence."

And according to that narrative, enemies of the congregation had lowered themselves to make untoward accusations about the founder as early as the 1950s. We heard that he had been accused of an addiction to painkillers, that he had engaged in questionable relationships with a young woman or two in Mexico, but each of these had its explanation: each was an attack, a lie aimed at discrediting Maciel and stopping the progress of the Legion. That narrative—of Maciel, the saintly founder, continually bearing the cross of defamation and inexplicable hatred, his lot in life as founder of this new work of God—was the very backbone of our self-understanding as a congregation.

So, in February 1997, by default, most Legionaries grappled to fit these new accusations into that narrative. I tried as well, and worked hard at it. Yet from that moment on, I struggled with periods of doubt about the congregation. I kept those doubts to myself for years, and my subconscious worked hard to bury them. But my faith in the congregation began to erode ever so slowly until its utter collapse twelve years later.

Meanwhile, the Legion published a statement vigorously denying the allegations and calling into question the motivations and moral integrity of the accusers. For my part, I did in fact seek as much information from the superiors as they were willing to give me about the whole situation, and particularly about the accusers.

My own interactions with Maciel had been limited in comparison with those of other Legionaries, never longer than an hour or two at a time, mostly while I was studying in Rome and later as a Legionary priest in New York. These were always in the company of at least a few others. Based on these experiences, and with my interior life nourished by reading spiritual letters we believed he had written, I thought I knew this man.[2] *And I loved him as a spiritual father.* We would refer to him as "*Nuestro Padre*," our father founder—an expression which, when in print, would always be written with a capital *N* and a capital *P*.

From 1997 onward and into the first years of my priesthood, and bolstered by my own psychological defense mechanisms, I worked hard at sustaining—both for myself and others—the grand narrative of our heroic founder and the divinely assisted establishment of the congregation. But so did the vast majority of Legionaries, including most of the superiors. In so doing, we were unwittingly keeping ourselves immersed in a kind of parallel universe: we were all protagonists in this great, providential work of God—our congregation. We were called "to build up the Legion" (*"hacer Legión"*). Such was the Kool-Aid we drank, and it was readily available.

 ☙

Seven long years would pass before the Holy See would reopen its investigation of Maciel in 2004[3] and determine, within the course of a months-long investigation, that the primary accusations against Maciel were credible, principally, that he had, in fact, engaged in sexual misconduct, including the sexual abuse of several of the Legion's first seminarians, and committed the canonical crime of giving sacramental absolution to at least one of the victims he abused.[4] A communiqué from the Vatican Press Office on May 19, 2006, read in part:

> After having submitted the results of the investigation to an attentive study, the Congregation for the Doctrine of the Faith, under the guide of its new Prefect, His Eminence Cardinal William Levada, decided—taking account of the advanced age of the Reverend Maciel and his delicate health—to renounce any canonical process and to invite the Father to a reserved life of prayer and penance, renouncing every public ministry. The Holy Father [Pope Benedict XVI] has approved these decisions.

After Maciel's death in 2008, there came more revelations: Maciel had, in fact, been addicted to painkillers for years and had enlisted a close circle of trusted Legionaries to obtain a steady supply of drugs for him. In addition to sexually abusing young seminarians, he had fathered at least three children: a daughter (by one woman) and two sons (by another woman). The latter two have alleged that Maciel sexually abused them as children.

Maciel was, in actuality, a colossally enigmatic individual—a sociopathic sexual omnivore who presented to a broader public the credible persona of a religious leader and reformer, friend of popes, and darling of much of the Roman curia, who secretively used the Catholic religious order he founded to feed his lusts.

Subsequently, Cardinal Joseph Ratzinger, later Pope Benedict XVI, ordered an "apostolic visitation" of the Legionaries in 2009—a close scrutiny of all Legionary houses of formation and apostolate conducted by a team of bishops appointed by the pope. Following that visitation, early in July 2010, Cardinal Velasio de Paolis was named papal delegate to the Legionaries of Christ to shepherd the congregation through a "process of profound re-evaluation" as mandated in a communiqué from the Holy See to the Legionaries in early May of that same year.

◯ℛ

Maciel had roused the suspicions of at least two major superiors as early as 2004. For its part, the Holy See, in May 2006 had already disciplined Maciel, consigning him to "a life of prayer and penance," the outcome of its own independent investigation of Maciel, completed in late 2005, which *had already deemed credible* the principal accusations made against him. Father Álvaro Corcuera (then general director of the Legionaries, who succumbed to a brain tumor in 2014) had been summoned to a meeting at the Vatican in March 2006 and was informed of this outcome.

From that moment on, every member of the congregation had a fundamental right to know the truth regarding their revered founder. Moreover, the very good of the Church demanded an immediate and transparent communication of these facts.

We know today that by the end of 2006, Corcuera had been presented with further, independent evidence that Maciel had fathered at least one child.[5] Yet it was not until late 2008 that Corcuera finally opted for a slow and overly cautious rollout of a watered-down and minimalized version of the founder's sordid life. But it was to be shared first only with the congregation's superiors; rank-and-file members of the congregation would be informed at some undetermined point in the future. It was a plan that would prove catastrophic.

In reality, for nearly three years Corcuera kept the vast majority of Legionaries and members of Regnum Christi—the Legion's lay apostolic movement—in the dark until the Legionary leadership was finally forced to publicly admit Maciel's guilt in late January 2009 as leaked details about his mistress and child were about to hit the press.

Nor did Corcuera desist during those same years from continuing to foster the cult of personality that had enveloped Maciel for decades. In his homily at Maciel's funeral Mass, Corcuera several times used expressions indicating his apparent conviction that Maciel was already enjoying his eternal reward in heaven: "Now he is receiving God's eternal embrace, something he always longed for," explained Corcuera. He then went on to paint a hagiographical account of the founder's final breath just as several priests were beginning to concelebrate Mass at his bedside: "We celebrated that Mass," affirmed Corcuera, "when he was already in heaven."

Yet, anyone who knew Corcuera would know very well that he did none of this out of malice. In reality, Álvaro Corcuera remains a tragic figure in the history of the Legionaries. A lifelong and childlike devotee of Maciel, Corcuera was handpicked by the founder to succeed him as general director of the congregation— bereft as Corcuera was of some of the most basic and essential qualities of governance. I can only think that his impossibly poor judgments were largely the fruit of his own interior bewilderment, confusion, and utter loss of good sense as the facts about Maciel came to light and the congregation began to implode.

In 2014, a newly elected director general of the Legionaries apologized for "hesitations and errors of judgment when setting out to inform the members of the congregation and others … which have increased the suffering and confusion of many." Yet those determinations were more than the result of inept leadership or unspeakably poor judgment on the part of Corcuera; they resulted from the deliberate intent on the part of some individuals within the Legionary leadership to keep rank-and-file members of the congregation in the dark. As well, it defies belief to think Corcuera was not guided by certain members of the Roman Curia, themselves the product of a mindset which, in a case such as Maciel's, held that "prudence" required silence, secrecy, and subterfuge in order to "avoid further scandal."[6] Further, it remains simply implausible that Maciel's closest collaborators for decades could not have known anything about his egregious behavior, or at least have serious suspicions about him, well prior to 2006.[7]

In the end, the Legionaries released an official statement to the press on February 3, 2009, that read in part:

> We have learned some things about our founder's life that are surprising and difficult for us to understand. We can confirm that there are some aspects of his life that were not appropriate for a Catholic priest.

What ensued in the coming days was a public-relations fiasco and a pastoral nightmare. In the final days of January, Legionary superiors had scrambled to break the news to priest members of the congregation. Thousands of stunned and bewildered Legionary supporters only became aware of the revelations from news accounts on February 3.

Their questions and demands for explanations were met, more often than not, by subterfuge aimed at minimizing the gravity of the crisis. For their part, Legionaries and members of Regnum Christi were expected to follow the Legion's customary ways of not externalizing negativity, not criticizing the superiors and directors, nor expressing negative emotions to anyone but their spiritual directors.

CR

In late January 2009 my own religious superior finally sat me down to confirm that the allegations were true.

I immediately went numb—there's no other way to explain what I felt.

Shortly after the Holy See's actions against Maciel in May 2006, I had ceased trying to account for it all as some kind of unique "cross" that God had permitted Maciel to bear. For three years, I struggled mightily to believe in my congregation, and to validate it in the eyes of the Church. Now, in the course of one conversation with my religious superior over a late supper at a local diner, my entire world was upended. The accusations were essentially true. In one moment of pristine and devastating clarity, I realized that for the better part of twenty-three years I had been caught up in a lie, in a massive deception of unprecedented proportions in the Church.

Within days a raw, emotional pain was setting in hard, pain like I had never felt before. At age forty-four, my life was turned upside down. Questions raced through my head: How could we have been so duped? How could the facts of Maciel's depravities been concealed from us for so long? What was God doing? How could God let this happen to us? How could he let it happen—*to me*?

CR

Before going any further, I am compelled to say a few things about the current situation of the Legionaries, and of so many persons who have been hurt in the wake of the whole Maciel affair, and about those who remain both in the Legion and in Regnum Christi.

My intention here, in sharing my story, is not to denigrate the Legionaries or Regnum Christi members who, as a religious family, continue their journey of discernment of God's will now, nearly a decade into the aftermath of the crisis that occasioned my own discernment and decision to part ways.

I write with the awareness that my story—although uniquely my own in so many respects—is only one of many personal stories that could and should be told, of hundreds of laymen and women whose lives were negatively impacted by their experience with the Legionaries and with the Regnum Christi movement.

I think of the hundred or more former confreres of mine and brother priests in the Legionaries, who, like me, since 2009 discerned that they should continue to follow Christ on a new path. My story, compared with theirs, has no particular drama attached to it meriting special attention. While we have all suffered significantly in our own ways, I am aware of some who have suffered much more and for a longer time than I have.

Stories could also be told of hundreds of other lay Catholics whose experience was different, who are convinced their spiritual lives were definitively enriched by the Legion and Regnum Christi, consecrated men and women, lay members of Regnum Christi and hundreds of Legionary priests whose lives, like my own, were catapulted into the storm, but who discerned a very different path—a call to remain part of the process of renewal and reform which the Church would require of them, who also suffered grievously, but who continue today in their commitments.

Admittedly, in the first years that followed my departure, which coincided with the Legion's mandatory process of internal reform, I published a few articles in Catholic periodicals that were highly critical of the Legion, of the role of the superiors during the time of crisis, and of the dysfunctional internal culture of the congregation.[8] I also raised difficult questions about the existence and validity of a putative institutional religious charism, and I wondered whether it would not be best—for all those implicated and for the good of the Church—if the Holy See were to suppress the congregation, essentially to shut it down.

No doubt, some things I wrote might have offended some Legionaries and their supporters. I can imagine that my departure from the congregation instilled a sense of abandonment and hurt in some of my former comrades. All of this was ultimately inevitable. I stand by what I wrote at the time, knowing that my intention was not malicious. Much of what I wrote needed to be said. I was playing a role that few of us could uniquely play—offering candid and very public criticism of the Legionaries from someone with knowledge of the internal life of the congregation who could help sustain the external pressure that was necessary to rupture the web of deceptions in which so many of the members remained engulfed, and help them face certain realities in ways that might allow for a genuine reform of the congregation.

I am grateful today that over time I have been able to renew contact with some of my former confreres for whom I continue to feel great affection. By God's grace, and notwithstanding the dysfunctionality in which we lived, I have no doubt that we truly were blessed to participate in and make a very real contribution to the New Evangelization. Jesus accepted and blessed our sacrifice and gift of self in the Legion. I pray for those who have continued in the congregation, not without continued concern for their well-being, and acutely aware that a full accounting for the sordid history of Maciel has never been given, nor adequately investigated.[9]

Finally, always present in my mind and heart while writing this book have been the victims of Maciel's sexual abuse. I think especially of the courageous nine men who came forward publicly in 1997 after previous efforts over a period of decades to inform the Holy See had been of no avail. By their perseverance, they have done an incalculable and lasting good to the Church, inciting all those involved to heed the demands of justice, particularly the call to transparency and accountability. While much of the entire Maciel affair still remains to be accounted for, and the Legionaries must continue to uncover, correct, and be transparent with regard to any other unsavory elements of their history, these men were catalysts in a cathartic process of liberating minds and hearts from a web of darkness and deception in the Church.

I have been saddened and ashamed that I did not believe their stories sooner. I ask their forgiveness for the ways, as a Legionary, I contributed to denigrating their good names by perpetuating hearsay and gossip about their supposedly twisted intentions. And, to all, I ask forgiveness for the ways in which, in my ignorance, I myself contributed to propagating the cult of personality surrounding Maciel, and to perpetuating the web of deceptions in which we were all trapped.

⚭

I had a lot of emotions to deal with as the crisis unfolded in February 2009. I worked through moments of repugnance, horror, anger, and rage. I couldn't get it out of my head that twenty-three years of my life—what seemed to me to have been *the best years of my life!*—had apparently been dedicated to a fiction. The sense of having been utterly betrayed was nearly overwhelming, and it fueled my rage.

Another emotion I grappled with was shame—shame at having been duped! Sure, I could say to myself as some people attempted to console me at the time: "Hey, don't feel bad; you're in good company. Maciel duped thousands of people—including Blessed Paul VI and St. John Paul II." But that did little to temper my sense of shame, embarrassment, or the gut-wrenching sense of loss and sense of indignation at having been had, at having been manipulated—*for over two decades of my life.* I had been violated in my intellect and in my spirit. I had been sucked into an elaborate web, a labyrinth of deception. Once in, it was nearly impossible to see my way out, until finally the walls of the labyrinth began to crumble. Over time, I have recognized this as one of my deepest wounds: the sense of personal violation.

CR

As the initial strong emotions eventually subsided, there loomed the fairly urgent task of discerning what God was directing me to do next in my life, since it was becoming overwhelmingly clear that remaining in the Legion was simply not an option.

This required me to look back, carefully, prayerfully, and objectively over the steps that had presumably led me to the Legionaries more than two decades earlier. While in many ways I felt afloat in a sea of uncertainty, I cannot say I felt in the dark. On the contrary, with the admission of the truth on the part of the superiors, it was as if my life was suddenly inundated by light that allowed me to see myself, my relationship with Jesus, *my reality* with an objectivity I had frankly been largely deprived of since I entered the Legionaries.

As I looked back on my life, trying to discern the immediate future, what remained pristinely clear in my heart was that I was first called to the priesthood well before I supposedly discerned a vocation to religious consecration with the Legionaries. I had been ordained a priest in 2000—but had lived the first nearly ten years of priesthood in growing tensions with my superiors. I was becoming more and more aware of problems with the internal culture of our congregation. Aspects of community life became almost unbearable. We were not what we presented ourselves to be. The congregation—not Christ and his Church—was treated as the be-all and end-all. For years I lived in frequent need of shoring up my faith in the "work of God," constantly seeking to validate, justify, and offer explanations for the Legion, for her apostolic works, her approach to formation and priesthood, her achievements—always against a headwind of sometimes withering criticism from outside the congregation.

So, my eventual discernment that Our Lord was moving me in the direction of diocesan priesthood cannot be simply attributed to the Maciel crisis; on the contrary, for years my roots in the Legion had been withering, and a movement toward separation was inevitable, especially as I was able to conclude over time that the "discernment process" that led me to enter and remain in the Legion was problematic and raised serious questions about its validity—a topic I will return to in chapter 8.

Ultimately, an excellent spiritual director, along with trusted and prudent friends outside of the congregation, including one American bishop, helped me through this period. I am forever indebted to that bishop for his patience, boundless kindness, prudence, and availability to me during the immediate days of the crisis. I was able to discern in short order that, regardless of the future of the Legionaries, they were about to embark on what appeared to be nothing less than a "re-foundation" of the congregation—and I was not called to be a part of that. I discerned that Our Lord was moving me in the direction of diocesan priesthood, a reality confirmed by my spiritual director, and by multiple other indications by which I understood Our Lord to be affirming my new direction.

I subsequently left the Legionaries in April 2009 and set out on the road toward my incardination in the Archdiocese of New York, where I had, in fact, lived and ministered during my first eleven years of priesthood. But even though my discernment process was concluding, the shockwave had now passed, and my immediate next steps were much clearer, my *interior healing* was only beginning. After a few months in my new life as a parish priest, I began telling myself I was "over it." I soon discovered that was little more than a defense mechanism. The trauma was deep, and the healing would take a lot longer than I could have imagined. Nor did I expect the turmoil that was coming or just how severely my commitment to the Church would be challenged.

♋

Notwithstanding the external appearances—I'm sure I seemed fine to everyone—by the summer of 2010 I was struggling internally as never before in my life. To be sure, I was seeing my spiritual director regularly, engaging in priestly ministry, preaching, celebrating the sacraments, praying, and feeling the support of some wonderful priest friends in the Archdiocese of New York. Yet, inside I felt as if I were slowly drowning.

Many aspects of day-to-day Church life—the bureaucracy and red tape, the hackneyed ways of parish ministry, the clericalism, gossip, cynicism, and negativity in the clergy—contributed to create in me a sense of loathing for almost anything Church-related. Sometimes, even at Mass, I felt as if I was just going through the motions. My homilies seemed hollow. And most difficult of all—I was assaulted at times by the hitherto unthinkable temptation to abandon priestly ministry altogether. When I looked inside sometimes, it seemed all I could find was aching, anger, emptiness, and an almost overpowering urge to flee, to be done with the whole thing, to go somewhere far away and start a new life.

There were moments when I was utterly numb, feeling at times as if I no longer loved the Church. In particular, I struggled profoundly with the sense that I had been hurt *by* the Church. I will never forget one morning in particular when, after celebrating Mass and after the Church had emptied out, I stood gazing at the beautiful stained-glass depiction of the Resurrection ablaze in the morning sunlight, and I asked myself: "Do I still believe that?"

In the summer of 2010, what was happening inside was that I was beginning to experience—*to feel*—the depths of my own wounds. Yet, that was actually the necessary first step toward healing. And that's when I began writing—literally as therapy for myself—what would eventually become this book. So my story, thankfully, does not end here. I will share more about it in the following chapters, particularly about how I found healing in the aftermath of this traumatic experience, and how Jesus led me to discover in my wounds an oasis of grace, and a call to a new mission.

℘

CHAPTER 2

Soul Murder

"Take sides. Neutrality helps the oppressor, never the oppressed.
Silence encourages the tormentor, never the tormented."

—Elie Weisel

I have not suffered the personal devastation of sexual abuse. My own personal heartbreak within the Church, as devastating as it was, pales in comparison to the raw betrayal and the unspeakable suffering of those subjected to this extreme form of physical, moral, and spiritual cruelty. Victims of sexual abuse, especially those who have suffered at the hands of Catholic priests, have been foremost in my mind and heart when writing this book and reflecting on those who have been hurt in the Church.

Soul Murder

Some 17,600 Americans have alleged they were abused by more than 6,500 clerics from 1950 to June 2015, according to a review of data by BishopAccountability.org. Many victims who were sexually abused by clergy as children refer to what they have suffered with a blunt and chilling expression. They call it *soul murder*. Many wait for years to open up to someone about the abuse. The reasons for this are often complex. They are afraid of not being believed;

they fear the reactions they will receive and how this knowledge will impact relationships with a spouse or child, with family or parishioners, or how it would be handled in the local news media. Yet when they do eventually begin sharing their stories, they discover that telling what happened, and being listened to and believed, is key to any possible healing. While victims are individually unique in their manner of handling the aftermath of their own abuse, most eventually want their stories acknowledged. For many, in fact, sharing their stories becomes a mission: they want to know if the perpetrator had other victims; they want those victims to know that they were not alone, that it is okay to come forward, that the abuse was not their fault.

Not "Them" and "Us"

As child sexual abuse expert Dr. Monica Applewhite shared with me, there is one enormous misperception that unfortunately shapes the attitudes of not a few Catholics toward the reality of clergy sexual abuse. "Persons who were abused are not *them*; they are *us*," she observed emphatically. "They came from the families who were closest to the Church: they worked and volunteered for the Church, they had a child who was considering becoming a priest or nun; these were people who spent a lot of time in the Church."

Part of the tragic story of the abuse crisis is that victims were seen as adversaries, not only by bishops and diocesan lawyers, but by fellow Catholics who held them suspect because their stories seemed too incredible and because—it was often assumed—they "just want to harm the Church." Victims of sexual abuse by the clergy are not the adversary, and as Dr. Applewhite observes, "When victims come forward with their stories, they are giving us the gift of truth." Here, too, the truth will set us free.

Facing the Reality

On a Sunday evening in late February 2016, I directed a screening and discussion for some thirty of our seminarians and faculty of the movie *Spotlight*, which recounts the story of how, in 2002, *The Boston Globe*'s "Spotlight" team of investigative reporters uncovered the massive scandal of child sexual abuse and coverup in the Boston Archdiocese. That same Sunday evening, *Spotlight* won the Oscar for best picture.

It was the second time I had seen *Spotlight*. In the movie's final scene, the Spotlight team is manning the phones in their office on the morning that their story broke in January 2002. The phones, in fact, are ringing off the hook. We are led to understand that the scores of callers are mostly victims of abuse who have been empowered by the story to come forward.

This is followed by a series of titles that appear on screen before the final credits roll: list upon list of the names of hundreds of U.S. dioceses and of dozens of countries where clergy sexual abuse has occurred, indicating the incomprehensible magnitude of the crisis. As happened the first time I saw *Spotlight*, I was again left hunched in my seat, barely restraining the tears.

Spotlight reopened for me that same gnawing feeling I had not felt in years—that "shitty feeling," as reporter Mike Rezendes puts it in one of the movie's most poignant scenes after he finally gets his hands on documents detailing that the Boston Archdiocese had knowledge of, and flagrantly mishandled and attempted to hide, child sexual abuse by members of its clergy.

That feeling Rezendes described is something most Catholics would rather not feel, and to which they would rather not expose themselves or their loved ones. And that's understandable, to an extent. There is a part of us that wants to keep the reality of clergy sexual abuse and its aftermath at a safe mental and emotional distance. The idea of sexual abuse of children is an acutely anxiety-provoking thought; and our minds naturally tend to filter and block such thoughts. This peculiar psychological dynamic has, in fact, shaped cultural attitudes toward sexual abuse for centuries, and in large part explains societal malaise and indolence in attempting to deal with and prevent child sexual abuse wherever it occurs.

So, naturally, Catholics recoil. While such dodging, distancing, and denial are understandable, they constitute fundamental obstacles to the Church's healing process, and ultimately to creating and sustaining within the Church the type of environments that are truly safe for children, as well as safe havens of support, nurture, and recovery for victims of abuse. For that to become a reality, we all need to listen to victims tell their stories.

Victims of sexual abuse—particularly abuse endured in childhood—can be vulnerable and fragile. Many suffer through lifelong, often daily, emotional and psychological battles. Many are diagnosed with post-traumatic stress disorder in all its cruelty: bouts with insomnia and nightmares, anxiety attacks, flashbacks, social isolation, depression, self-destructive behaviors.

The victims who were willing to speak with me in some manner—these remarkable and courageous men and women—have taught me one simple thing: we who have not suffered the torture of sexual abuse *really have no idea what victims have gone through*.

So in my mind there is no more adequate way to come to grips with the horror experienced by survivors of sexual abuse than by hearing their stories—not in snippets filtered through the news media, but rather, if at all possible, in person, up close, in their own words, catching their gestures, looking into their eyes, hearing their voice.

Jean's Story

Sadly, accounts of clergy sexual abuse recounted in disturbing detail have not been lacking online and in the news media. Survivors of abuse—not exclusively, but typically, males—have mustered extraordinary courage in sharing their stories. Each story is as unique as each victim of abuse. I could have easily incorporated elements of their stories into this book, but as I made progress on the manuscript I was blessed to meet and interview a remarkable Catholic woman we will call Jean. Jean too is a survivor of clergy sexual abuse. Thirty-nine years of her life passed before she finally felt the courage to report her abuser to authorities in her diocese, well after the perpetrator was dead. By the time we met, she felt ready to go public for the first time with her story, agreeing to do so in the pages of my book.

Our interview lasted nearly three hours. In what follows, I have quoted large portions of our conversation as well as portions of some of her written testimonials and woven them into a narrative. While not simply a transcription of our interview, this does represent a faithful account of her story as she shared it with me. Jean only requested that her identity should remain anonymous, as well as that of her perpetrator—we'll call him Father Bill. In order to comply with her request, I have altered the details of the setting in which her story unfolds. Those alterations do not in the least alter the content of her personal story.

Jean's abuse happened when she was between the ages of fourteen and twenty, in the late sixties into the early seventies, and her allegations have been deemed credible by authorities within the diocese where her abuse occurred.

Why she did not report the abuse sooner will become clear.

How grace has triumphed through her darkness will also become readily evident.

This is Jean's story.

ଔ

Jean is in her mid-sixties and still radiates a kind of farm-girl wholesomeness. She is quick to smile, her eyes are bright, and she expresses herself spontaneously with small-town simplicity. It did not take long to discover in her a vast reservoir of spiritual depth and insight emerging from her personal experience of repeated sexual abuse. She bore the hurt for nearly forty years until the recurring nightmares were too much for her. Her personal tragedy did not stop her from becoming a nurse, marrying, and raising a family.

Jean began our meeting by showing me her first Communion photo taken with her classmates, the girls in dainty white first Communion dresses, the boys with meticulously combed hair in their white suits. Father Bill, the proud pastor—in his cassock, with hands folded reverently—stood behind them, beaming for the photo, flanked at right and left by altar boys. Jean identified herself and her twin brother for me. Then, referring to Father Bill, she explained: "This priest baptized me. He heard my first confession. He gave me my first Communion, and he buried my little sister." Father Bill was the priest at the altar when Jean and her husband were united in marriage. He had been a priest at Jean's parish— most of the time as its pastor—for more than forty-seven years until he eventually retired in the local community.

And in such a small community—Norman Rockwellian in its wholesomeness and simplicity—it was no surprise that Father Bill was a celebrity. His long years as pastor gave him a kind of mythical stature. He was a constant presence in the local media and had an in with most community leaders.

The parish also had a beautiful Marian shrine on the property that Jean absolutely loved. The parish church, offices, grounds, and shrine required a small body of employees to whom Father Bill offered a generous daily wage. He was especially fond of hiring teenage girls.

ଔ

The summer Jean turned fourteen, Father Bill personally invited her to join the staff. Jean was thrilled. Her pious Catholic upbringing had instilled in her a lively faith, and a profound veneration for her pastor, who, although not a regular presence in Jean's home, had nonetheless been very close to the family. The first sexual assault occurred on her second day on the job. Jean recounts:

> The second day of my employment, he entered the tiny building where [I was working]. He pushed me back to the counter and thrust his tongue into my mouth.
>
> I gagged.
>
> It tasted so bad from pipe and cigar tobacco. I thought I was going to vomit, but I didn't. I remember thinking: If you slap a priest, do you go to hell? I didn't know what to say or do. He just turned around and walked out. The abuse continued and worsened. I told him to stop, but he continued to abuse me. He was forty-five and I was fourteen. That's how it started.

Eventually Father Bill would rationalize the abuse by chiding Jean, saying he didn't want her to be a "cold fish" when she got married. He also pointed out to her that another teenage girl who had worked before Jean's time at the parish had, unlike Jean, "responded well" to Father Bill's treatment of her. As Jean explains, Father Bill sought out every possible opportunity to abuse her:

> About once a month Father Bill would take the group of four or five teens who worked for him to a nearby movie theater after closing. I didn't want to go. My work uniform was a blue skirt and a white blouse. No matter where I sat, he made sure that he moved people so that he could sit next to me. He would always sit on my left side, which allowed him to move his right hand from my knee to my thigh, and then to my underpants. I felt like, "What's wrong with me—that he does it to me and not to everybody else?"

When I was fifteen years old Father Bill called my parents
one evening to say that he would take me home after work
that night, saving them the long trip to town. What he
didn't tell them was that he was planning on stripping me
of my blouse and bra, and touching me. And as always he
put his tongue in my mouth. When we finally got home,
he sat down at our dining room table and ate homemade
chocolate-chip cookies and drank coffee with my mom
and dad while I cried in my room.

The abuse went on for six years. As she grew older, the episodes
took on more of the character of attacks—a word Jean used several
times in our interview. She would often end up going home with
nicks, scratches, and bruises:

> Only once did I think he was going to rape me. He stopped
> before it got to that point. He was noticeably shaken by
> what he had attempted to do. I can't tell you how many
> times he attacked me. And yet, there is a part of me that
> respected him; he was a priest.

ॐ

For the perpetrator, on a very deep psychological level, abuse is
about power, control, and self-affirmation. Father Bill seems to
have been no exception, and perhaps it should not surprise us that
he went so far as to use sacramental confession to manipulate Jean
into believing that she—not he—was the guilty party:

> One of the things that he did—I never understood at
> the time how bad it was—he would come to me and say,
> "I'm going to hear confessions now; would you like to
> come? I think it's a good time for you to go." So I would
> go. And I would say, "Bless me, Father, for I have sinned."

And from then on, I never said a word. He told me all the sins I had committed. And I didn't even understand what those words meant. And I was like—okay, he was there; he knows; he's the priest. He said my sins were forgiven, and I left. And I would pray my three Our Fathers, three Hail Marys, and three Glory Bes.

Jean observed that such sacrilegious confessions happened more than once:

And he didn't take any responsibility for what had happened. He didn't say, "Oh, I shouldn't have done this." He never, ever apologized. Ever. He never once said, "Oh, that was wrong." Never.

ભ

In addition to the sexual abuse Jean endured, there were many other hurts. When her father passed away, for example, Father Bill came to the funeral home to lead the family and friends in prayer. At one point he invited Jean to approach the casket and kneel with him on the kneeler. She watched, horrified, as Father Bill extended his hand and gruffly smacked the folded hands of the cadaver four or five times: "You were a good man, Jim." The slapping motions smeared away enough makeup to expose the blackened skin of Jean's father's folded left hand. Jean broke down into uncontrollable sobs, but never said a word. Reflecting back on such a painful episode today, Jean sees it as one more instance of how this priest "could never, ever, keep his hands where they belonged."

Ultimately, after Father Bill's death, he was buried in the cemetery in proximity to her mom and dad; she had to walk past his tombstone on the way to her parents' graves. She could not get away from this man, it seemed:

I was so mad ... and what came to my mind was: if I would vomit on his tombstone, would my stomach acid be strong enough to erase his name? So nobody would know who he is. Why did he have to be buried there? It just wasn't right.

It would take most of Jean's adult life, much prayer, and much patience to finally receive the grace of forgiving her perpetrator.

ര

After listening to Jean for some time as she related, in painful detail, her experiences of repeated sexual assaults, I asked why she hadn't quit her job. After all, it was the job that occasioned the abuse. Her answer, in part, was quite simple: she loved her job.

But to understand what she meant, you have to understand that it wasn't a job for her, even though she was paid a dollar an hour—for the times, a considerable amount of money for a teenager. And while that was undoubtedly important to her, in the long run it didn't matter in comparison to the connection with God that she found in the parish church, and particularly at the Marian shrine:

My faith grew there. I absolutely fell in love with God. And I really felt how much he loved me. I mean, he loved us so much.... And he sent his Son ... and Jesus was God! And he died. And he would have died just for me. And he would have died just for you.... He loved each one of us that much. So, religion wasn't something I just knew; it became something very internal with me. And there was nothing Father Bill could do to take that away.

Another question I posed to her—as anyone might be tempted to ask—was why she didn't seek help. Here the answer is a bit more complex, and here is where those of us who have not been victims of sexual abuse must set aside our "logic" and "common sense," and try to enter the mind and heart of a person who has lived in the grip of paralyzing fear, a fear which began as a child and persisted into adulthood.

Jean's was the fear that her parents would find out about the abuse, and what the consequences might be, not only for her family but also for the tiny close-knit community in which they lived. In particular, she feared that Father Bill's guilt would get the better of him, and he would one day go to her parents (he had retired only blocks from them) and confess the whole thing to them.

Jean explained that on one occasion news had gotten around town about a teenage girl in a neighboring town who had become pregnant out of wedlock. Her parents had "sent her away." Jean asked her mother if she thought that had been the right thing to do, and her mother responded affirmatively without hesitation. That response was like pouring gasoline onto the fire of a fear that was already raging inside Jean:

> And I really thought they would send me away too. And where would I go? What would happen to me? I could be wrong ... but in my opinion I believe [my parents] would have blamed me completely. Everything was kind of black and white [for them] and they followed the rules, and that would not have been allowed. Looking back, I maybe could've talked to my dad. But I think it would have torn our family apart.

This fear engulfed Jean well into her adult life until Father Bill's death. As for her husband, whom she adored and with whom she shared forty years of marriage until his death, she could only tell him a little. Her husband adored Father Bill. "My husband knew a little bit, and he did not want to know more," Jean explained. "And I respected that."

CR

But there were other attempts to get help. She would sometimes confide to a priest in confession—because this was the only place she felt halfway safe and confident mentioning it. Yet, she was often sorely disappointed:

> Most priests aren't good there. They say, "Get over it" and "You need to forgive him" and "What's wrong with you?" And what happens is you just don't go back. They don't say, "I'm sorry it happened." But what they say most often is, "Get over it." No one says it nicely. My pain is not with what happened—I mean, it was ugly and it hurt me—but my biggest complaint is with how the clergy handles it … because they don't know what to do with me.

As the abuse went on through the 1960s, Jean got another idea:

> I got to the point where I was going to call the bishop. I thought that would work. But I didn't have the bishop's phone number. And if I went home and dialed and tried to get the number, there would be a charge on our phone bill. And Mom knew every bill. And then I got to thinking that I couldn't call him anyway because we were on a party line. And everybody would listen [to each other's calls]. You would hear this click when they picked up the phone.

Once when Jean was fifteen, she did reach out to a priest in a nearby town. But consistent with the times, this priest, though very kind, did nothing more than encourage Jean to "protect" herself, to "stay close to the doors" so she could avoid or escape Father Bill. It never crossed his mind to report Jean's abuse to the police. For all Jean knows, he never confronted Father Bill. His words were kind, but he did nothing to prevent further abuse. "He didn't know any better," Jean reflected. "The world was different."

CR

There is a part of Jean's story that in many ways struck me as more painful to listen to than the details of her abuse—because it is a part of her hurting that was needless, impossibly callous, and mindlessly inflicted upon her by yet another priest to whom she first turned, well over thirty years after she was abused, in a first moment of vulnerability as she sought compassion and understanding.

As Dr. Applewhite explains, when an abuse victim first opens up and is vulnerable with another person about the fact of the abuse, the reaction the victim receives is of critical importance—and positive or negative, it imprints on the psyche of the victim.

When, as an adult woman well into her fifties, Jean first opened up to a priest outside of confession—one of her own parish priests—about her abuse, after going into some detail about Father Bill's assaults on her, the priest became visibly agitated and finally blurted out: "You scare me.... *You* scare me!"

Jean was nonplussed.

"I know what people like *you* do to priests," he snapped, "you make wild accusations and pretty soon we're all suspect. So you can just stay away. I don't want to have anything to do with you!"

Jean attempted to explain that she was not accusing him or much less all priests, but he cut her off. What then followed, in Jean's state of defenseless vulnerability, was unimaginably insensitive, and would leave her tender conscience needlessly engulfed in turmoil for a long time to come. "And by the way," the priest retorted, "supposing what you're saying is true, what was *your part* in this?"

CR

Jean shared her story with me for a number of reasons, but principal among them was that she wanted me to be able to communicate to priests—and seminarians—how *not* to treat a victim of sexual abuse who opens up to them in counseling or the confessional.

I asked Jean what she would say to other victims of sexual abuse:

Number one: what he did to you was not your fault. And I'm sorry it happened. That was all I wanted to hear. Rather than being told, "You scare me, and you're a liar."

Jean did not report her abuse to the diocese until well after Father Bill had died. She recalled how, when the diocesan review board was going to examine her accusation, she sought to speak to them in person. This was vitally important to her:

I wanted to be there when that panel met ... I wanted them to know that what they were doing was valid and important in the Church.

Today, Jean continues to heal. The abundant spiritual healing she has already received, she acknowledges, came not without setbacks, periods of discouragement, and struggles. She shared that eventually it was after fervent prayer to the Holy Spirit that she finally received relief: she was able to forgive Father Bill, and the nightmares abruptly ended.

℞

When I interviewed Jean, she made it clear that her ability to forgive her perpetrator was a gift that was nearly forty years in coming, something superhuman, something she could not do on her own. She had only very recently gotten to that place. "I want him to be in heaven," she insisted, referring to Father Bill. And she hopes to see him there one day.

What is particularly remarkable about Jean—and so tragically differs from the personal stories of many other victims—is how her Catholic faith, her *faith and trust in the Church*, remained intact, notwithstanding years of sexual abuse. And the goodness—the genuine spiritual charity—she directs today toward her perpetrator no doubt leaves the reader (as it left me) off balance.

I was angered by her story. Incensed. Shaken.

The reader can't help but ask: *How could she, in her right mind, possibly want this man to be in heaven?* Is she still in some sort of denial? And how is it that she did not lose her faith, that she did not walk away from the Church? We'll have occasion to explore and answer these questions, and return to Jean's story, in chapter 8.

As a closing thought, it is to be hoped that Jean's home diocese where the abuse occurred will eventually make the option to publicize *all* the names of accused priests from the diocese with credible allegations against them, even if the allegations came to light only after the offending cleric was deceased. Such a policy corresponds quite simply to a fundamental requirement of justice. To be forthcoming in this way, as Dr. Applewhite has pointed out, is to provide the Church with the gift of truth. And in the matter of clergy sexual abuse, the Church's absolute transparency is the gift we can ill afford to deny future generations of Catholics.

CHAPTER 3

⚮

A Heart-to-Heart
about Catholic Priests

"Accept from the holy people of God the gifts to be offered to Him.
Know what you are doing, and imitate the mystery you celebrate:
model your life on the mystery of the Lord's cross."

—From the Rite of Priestly Ordination

Where to begin?

In light of the preceding chapter, it bears repeating that by far the vast majority of Catholic priests have never sexually abused anyone. Our thoughts should turn to that throng of priests, past and present, who have sought to live in earnest fidelity to the commitments they made the day of their ordination, priests who have striven for genuine holiness against great odds and amidst countless obstacles.

So, dare I begin this chapter with an expression of gratitude? That may sound self-serving, as I am a Catholic priest. But take it rather as the expression of my own lifelong admiration for these men who in so many ways have been my personal heroes, and who rendered me the greatest service a human person could ever offer by placing me sacramentally and existentially in touch with the Mystery of Christ.

Priests can also be, in very personal, often undisclosed ways, some of the most hurting persons in the Church today—much more than most of our lay brothers and sisters can imagine.

At the top of the list we would have to locate the reality of false accusations of sexual misconduct against priests who see their good name trampled upon and destroyed.[10] Up there as well are the chasms of distrust that have opened up between priests and their bishops in the last decade. This has been an unintended but very real side effect of the bishops' efforts to implement new policies for handling allegations of sexual abuse against priests over the past decade and a half.

Closely related we would have to acknowledge the low priestly morale in some dioceses that is seldom effectively addressed; the dysfunctionality inherent in too many chancery offices; the attitude of some bishops who treat their priests as something less than collaborators in ministry, who are distant, calculating, and utilitarian, who treat their priests with an air of suspicion. I think, for example, of an archbishop (and later cardinal) who once, in rendering a legal deposition over abuse cases in his archdiocese, explained to the lawyers that the relationship of the priests to the archdiocese was not unlike that of "private contractors" to a corporation. The archbishop was obviously reaching for an analogy that the lawyers might understand, but the choice of analogies was revealing.

It has often struck me as well that referring to priests as "personnel"—although commonplace in most dioceses, as in "office of priest personnel" or "priest personnel board"—suggests that a bureaucratized, corporate mentality has come to characterize and dominate the internal cultures of our chanceries. It's a far cry from a very different model suggested to us in the New Testament, that of the presbyters gathered with their bishop and the local community of disciples in prayer (see Acts 20:17-38).

Beyond these forms of hurt, there are the ubiquitous faults, deficiencies, and quirks that sadly pervade the internal culture of communities of priests themselves: the intrigue, backbiting, politics, oneupmanship, envy, and turf wars; the loneliness and lack of genuine fraternal interest in one another; the feeding off one another's cynicism.

There is the constant burden of parish ministry, often without adequate priest collaborators; the thousand worries of shepherding a parish community, the never-ending uncertainties about the future, and at times the bleakness of a parish landscape that seemingly shows no signs of fruit for all our labors. And, of course, there's a priest's own personal and intimate struggles, ill health, and hardships.

Of course, if we are bluntly honest, priests are often the cause of much hurting in the Church today. I say it as a priest who knows that, in my own actions and omissions, failures and sinfulness, I too have hurt members of the Church.

In this chapter, I do not pretend to embark on a comprehensive assessment of the struggles of Catholic priests, the ways in which they hurt others and are hurting individuals themselves. Much less do I attempt an in-depth analysis of the current state of the Catholic priesthood. Rather, I simply want to offer the reader and my brother priests some candid reflections on several issues in priestly life today as they come to bear on the reality of a hurting Church.

The Universal Call

Of late it has become awkward to talk or write about holiness, as if it's just not "PC," as if it were condescending, judgmental, arrogant, insensitive, out of touch, antiquated—or all of the above. Well, please bear with me. I'm convinced that some reflection on the holiness to which priests are called is exactly the right way to focus the reflections that will follow. And to that end, we have to begin by remembering that it is still the case today that all people, all of us, are called by God to holiness.

The emphasis on that *universal* call was, in fact, a hallmark of the Second Vatican Council. Its Dogmatic Constitution on the Church affirms:

> Strengthened by so many and such great means of salvation, all the faithful, whatever their condition or state— though each in his own way—are called by the Lord to that perfection of sanctity by which the Father himself is perfect.[11]

The Catholic who, by God's grace, strives earnestly to live in that genuine interior freedom we call the "state of grace"—that is, a life characterized by the absence of deliberate concessions to mortal sin—this Catholic is, indeed, holy, in a real, albeit imperfect (not yet complete), way. We might call such a state a first degree of holiness, even if characterized by struggles, and by plenty of deliberate falls in matters less serious. Such a person might not seem holy according to certain pietistic standards, but there is genuine sanctity present in such a person nonetheless, in possession as they are of the necessary foundation on which greater personal sanctity can be built.

The same applies to priests.

Not surprisingly, the council's Decree on the Ministry and Life of Priests emphasizes, in turn, the special way that priests are called to respond to that *same* universal invitation:

> Like all other Christians they have received in the sacrament of Baptism the symbol and gift of such a calling and such grace that even in human weakness they can an must seek for perfection, according to the exhortation of Christ: "Be you therefore perfect, as your Heavenly Father is per-

fect" (Mt 5:48). Priests are bound, however, to acquire that perfection in special fashion. They have been consecrated by God in a new manner at their ordination and made living instruments of Christ the Eternal Priest that they may be able to carry on in time his marvelous work whereby the entire family of man is again made whole by power from above.[12]

Pope St. John Paul II, in his apostolic exhortation *Pastores Dabo Vobis*, reiterated and summarized this teaching, synthesizing the two realities and emphasizing their complementarity: the entire people of God is called to holiness and to share in the priesthood of the people of God; those ordained to the ministerial priesthood are called to holiness in a "special way" proper to their state and deriving from the priesthood, but for the service and sanctification of the people of God.

I think this is the proper context within which to understand why the lay faithful instinctively and correctly expect more of priests, and hold us to a higher standard of morality. They expect their priests to lead by example.

And it's no secret that the best single catalyst for vocations to the priesthood is the personal holiness of those who have already embraced the call. Young men are attracted to the priesthood first and foremost by the holiness of the priests they have known—a fact borne out in just about every vocation story.

Yet, it's an expectation that must be imbued with the realism that we—priests—are all too human. And just like our lay brothers and sisters, we are imperfect, often and in many ways broken, and we must often deal with trials and tribulations that are quite unique to our condition as priests.

The Surprising Contours of a Holy Priestly Life

In the final moment of the Rite of Priestly Ordination, at the presentation of the gifts at the altar, the bishop in turn presents the newly ordained priest with the paten and chalice. The bishop entreats him: "Accept from the holy people of God the gifts to be offered to Him. Know what you are doing, and imitate the mystery you celebrate: model your life on the mystery of the Lord's cross."

In other words, once upon a time in our lives we priests made a commitment to pursue genuine holiness of life, and to strive—amid our own struggles and sinfulness—to remain faithful to that commitment through a life of ongoing conversion, a life that would ordinarily include daily personal prayer time, daily celebration of the Eucharist, Marian devotion, an annual retreat, and regular spiritual direction. Their presence in the life of a priest is certainly a hopeful indicator that he is striving after holiness.

But beyond these indicators, how would an average Catholic recognize genuine priestly holiness? By what standards do you assess it? I am taking for granted, of course, that the laity has a genuine stake in the holiness of their priests; they rightly expect it, and are not mistaken to look for signs of holiness of life. It is possible to do so without acting judgmentally. My point, however, is that it is very easy to miss genuine holiness in a priest, especially when more superficial pietistic criteria are in play.

To be sure, the truest indicators of genuine holiness are often unavailable to external observation. Add up all the observable elements you want: "Father is such a good preacher," "Father is so reverent at the altar," "Father visited my dad in the hospital and got him to go to confession," "Father is so dedicated to the homeless shelter," "Father celebrates the Latin Mass," "Father wears the cassock on Sundays," and so on. It certainly does not follow from this that "Father is a holy priest." These externals may or may not be confirmations of genuine holiness of life because, again, that holiness is really determined by elements that often elude the common categories by which certain individuals evaluate their priests. Now obviously we really can't speak of genuine holiness in a priest who habitually and callously exposes himself to moral hazards, allowing his conscience to become clouded, and conceding to what he knows to be sinful behaviors, particularly in matters of chastity, or in conduct that—given one's own peculiar temperament and struggles—could soon become addictive. That being said, there are priests who have been down this road, *but have repented*, and today lead exemplary lives.

I think as well of beloved brother priests who, for a diverse set of reasons and circumstances, one day found themselves struggling with an addiction and were forced to confront it, who were sent for treatment and today are in recovery thanks to their humility, honesty, hard work, fidelity to a wellness plan, and exercise of accountability to their bishop. Today they are priests who capitalize on their own experience of weakness so as to counsel, guide, and encourage others in similar struggles.

Again, according to certain pietistic standards, such priests might not "seem" very holy—which is just to evince the superficiality of such standards. The priest who struggles mightily with his own foibles, who has regular recourse to the Sacrament of Penance, who prays as best he can, who bears all of this for love of God and for the people of God, *who bears all of this with genuine humility*—this is a truly holy priest.

Indeed, one can't insist enough that among the best indicators of priestly holiness of life are things that often escape external observation: Is this man genuinely humble? Does he live with profound interior detachment from himself, from others, from what he has, and from what he does? Does this man *pray*? Does this priest have a vibrant commitment to seek intimate union with Jesus Christ?

The priest cannot give what he does not have. If I am empty of Jesus interiorly, I will inevitably end up offering the people of God not Jesus but simply myself. My interior life will be filled not with light, inspiration, growing virtue, patience, and pastoral vibranc but with what Thomas Merton so aptly described as the "warm darkness" of one's own sensible nature.[13]

Tragically, some priests end up there—in the muck of self-absorption, cynical, living in spiritual mediocrity, their personal covenantal relationship with Jesus in tatters. And this constitutes a great suffering for the entire Mystical Body of Christ.

How, one rightly asks, does a priest end up like this?

Some priests just succumb to cynicism: cynicism about the Church and about their own possibilities for fidelity and holiness. Maybe it was the result of a midlife crisis; maybe it started early on in their ministry; maybe it had already begun in seminary. It is essentially a capitulation to discouragement: the bar seems too high; dreams of a faithful, honest, holy priestly life seem like youthful illusions. Maybe Father has lived for so long, so vexed by temptations and struggles, including the seemingly insurmountable peculiarities of his own temperament, that he essentially throws in the towel.

In so doing, a priest settles for so much less than what he is called to be and become. Beyond the veneer of affability, he harbors a profound dissatisfaction with himself. He allows himself to get to the point where he does not have a prayer life to speak of, he neglects praying the breviary, chastity becomes more and more problematic, as do the temptations of alcohol and other unhealthy habit-forming behaviors. He does not have a spiritual director and goes for months on end without approaching confession. And he can go like this for years, and even for the span of an entire priesthood. Mediocrity in the priesthood has always been present in the Church, and likely always will be; yet it never ceases to occasion great spiritual harm to the Mystical Body.

While many priests in this sad condition can and do manage to reach retirement in such a state, I believe that more fall to the wayside. For most, perseverance in the priesthood in such an interior state is hardly tenable. A man who simply does not pray; who allows deliberate infidelities in chastity and celibacy; who fills his interior with anger, cynicism, and criticism of everyone and everything in the diocese (beginning with, but certainly not limited to, the bishop) with off-color humor, with unhealthy and worldly television and film; who does not seek priestly fraternity; such a man might never actually abandon the priesthood, but his ministry will remain passive—and largely fruitless.

That's why another less than obvious indicator of personal holiness in a priest is his *endurance and perseverance* in active *and faithful* ministry, especially when this has entailed years of all kinds of adversity—internal and external. I am speaking here of long years of frequent, hard, gritty—and *often unseen and unnoticed*—acts of virtue: endless acts of keeping one's composure, holding one's tongue, sustaining positive thoughts, giving the world a pleasant semblance and a smiling face while interiorly traversing untold turmoil, the ongoing exercise of patience, giving the benefit of the doubt, forgiving, gritting one's teeth and just bearing it again and again. This is especially true of my brother priests (and they are the majority) who have lived and will live out their priesthood in *parish ministry*.

At this often-overlooked level of the priest's life, the grace of ordination bears fruit again and again, and the careful observer can discover the vibrant presence and action of the Holy Spirit. Consistency and integrity of priestly life, enduring over years and years—here we have a true indicator of a rather profound degree of personal holiness, of the action of grace and an intense relationship with Our Lord.

What I have described here is what I see and sense in so many of my brother priests. Truly, the Church is blessed with a majority of priests (and bishops) who are genuinely striving for holiness of life, striving to *model their lives on the mystery of the Lord's cross.*

Certainly, we have our shortcomings and failures and quirks. But last time I checked, so did just about every saint.

Clericalism

"Clericalism" in the Catholic Church is not easy to define, yet most priests, at least, know what we mean by it. Like pornography—to borrow the famous dictum—it's hard to define, but you know it when you see it. And if we've been paying attention to Pope Francis, we know he doesn't like clericalism, and he doesn't hesitate to impugn it. In fact, he unflinchingly and spontaneously connects clericalism with much of the hurting that is going on in the Church:

> This new era we have entered, and the many problems in the Church—like the poor witness given by some priests, problems of corruption in the Church, the problem of clericalism, for example—have left so many people hurt, left so much hurt.[14]

And where genuine holiness of life is absent, often some form of clericalism will be growing in its stead.

In my mind, a clericalist is a priest who, once ordained, indulges in the pursuit of power, pride, and perks. He does not seek to serve, but to be served. Consumed by an entitlement mentality, he lives absorbed in his pitiable self. We know it when we encounter it, and we rightly find it revolting: he is a priest by ordination, yes, but no longer in spirit, whose personality exudes a lust for power—and not infrequently lusts for other things.

Clericalist clergy can be found at both extremes of a conservative-progressive spectrum as well as dead center. Their theology can be steeped in a putative love of liturgical tradition; their theology can be loose and liberal. What they have in common is a sense of distinction and superiority vis-à-vis the laity, as if "taken from among men" (Heb 5:1) meant being set on a pedestal. The common priesthood of the faithful and the ministerial priesthood are, in truth, essentially different. But the clericalist treats the former as if it were nothing more than a quaint metaphor, and the latter as if it meant entry into an entitled caste.

Priestly ministry is a gift and a privilege, not a right. And those of us ordained to the ministerial priesthood in the Catholic Church have been blessed beyond comprehension to share in it. And this too is why we are mistaken—as we are sometimes prone to do—to put a possessive adjective before "priesthood" when speaking about it, as in "*my* priesthood" or "*his* priesthood." We have no grounds—none whatsoever—to lay claim to it as something that is "ours," our own, as a privilege, or a status symbol, or as something we have earned. Because it's not *our* priesthood; what we've been given, rather, is a share in the one priesthood of Jesus Christ.

Celibacy and Sexually Active Priests

My sense is that some priests, while celibate (the state of remaining unmarried for the sake of the kingdom of heaven) and avoiding sexual intimacy with others, often capitulate to discouragement or rationalization (or both) with regard to the broader issue of chastity. All Christians are called to achieve the virtue of chastity, whether single, married, or celibate. The *Catechism of the Catholic Church* beautifully defines chastity not in the negative—in terms of denial of sexual pleasure—but in the positive as "the successful integration of sexuality within the person and thus the inner unity of man in his bodily and spiritual being" (2337). Nevertheless, that does entail for the priest (and for anyone who takes a vow of perpetual chastity) a commitment to refrain for the rest of one's life from any deliberate sexually gratifying behavior as an expression of a single-hearted love for Christ and his Church, and of our total dedication to the people of God.

If all goes well, a priest's life of chaste celibacy becomes an expression of genuine interior freedom and habitual self-mastery. That's what the successful integration of one's sexuality would involve.

Of course, fidelity to such a commitment is possible only with God's grace and with the charism of celibacy, a special gift God freely offers the men and women he has called to consecrate their lives totally to him through that commitment. And faithfulness can be a battle at different periods of life; there can be long stretches of clear sailing and interior serenity; and there can be shorter or longer periods of struggle. If we stumble and have failures, we are strengthened by the sacraments, especially the Sacrament of Penance.

But the struggles and periodic failures that are part and parcel of living the virtue of chastity certainly do not render the commitment to celibacy impossible, nor do most priests experience either as an intolerable burden. I think most priests (certainly not all, but I dare say a majority) would tell you that the struggle is ultimately a good struggle, one we are all the better for, one that keeps us humble, human, and aware of our need for grace, a struggle we even come to love because through it we grow in our love for Jesus.

Yet, as mentioned, *all Christians* are called to live the virtue of chastity within their state in life. In light of Christian moral teaching and understanding of the human person, the marriage of one man and one woman is the only context within which the human person can properly pursue sexual expression, gratification, and union in a truly fulfilling way. All other persons, clergy and laity alike, who live outside of the bond of a valid marriage, are called to pursue and live the virtue of chastity and to embrace the Church's teaching on all issues of sexual morality, including the very personal issue of masturbation.[15]

Priests who have failed to embrace the specific teachings on sexual morality have possibly never understood the Church's holistic understanding of the human person, human love, and human sexuality, especially as articulated in Pope St. John Paul II's "theology of the body," or they have simply rejected it.

And this segues to the great harm occasioned in the Church by priests who deliberately choose behaviors that are blatantly contrary to their professed commitment to celibacy and to the virtue of chastity.

What percentage of Catholic clergy is currently sexually active—whether heterosexually or homosexually—or has been at least once with a consenting adult is next to impossible to know.[16] Most experts who have studied the phenomenon agree that it is not a large percentage of priests. Most priests I know would likely venture to guesstimate, as I do, that in dioceses in the United States, at least 5 to 10 percent of the clergy in any given diocese are sexually active with consenting adults or have been at least once post-ordination, including with other priests, at any given time. Are there dioceses with a higher incidence? Probably, yes, sad to say. Are there dioceses with a much lesser incidence? I would hope so.

Part of the problem is that the phenomenon of clerical sexual activity has been long shrouded—understandably—in secrecy, and is normally only divulged and addressed publicly as a scandal. Not that it is not scandalous—given the profound personal inconsistencies entailed and revealed in the priests in question—but it is precisely for this reason that sexually active clerics keep their sexual lives secret or at least try to, with the possible exception of the confessional.

That being said, a bishop certainly cannot passively acquiesce to such a status quo. His knowledge of sexually active priests in his diocese will more often than not be greatly limited and circumstantial at best. There will be hearsay and rumors about some of his priests. But he must endeavor as best he can, notwithstanding the limitations, to identify these troubled priests in his diocese if possible, to restrict their ministry if necessary, but most of all to get them the help they need to reorder their lives.

But, ah—there's the rub. Who will help them reorder their lives? Who is reaching out to them? Are we priests willing to go the extra mile and accompany a brother priest whose life is in tatters? Are there good Samaritans for these hurting brothers of ours? Or do we—priests and laity alike—simply dismiss them in condemnation once the rumors are confirmed? Do we care enough even to pray for all those priests who, in their own way, live in one of those "peripheries" of the Church, to borrow an image so dear to Pope Francis? Priests who live in an invisible margin, priests in trouble, priests whose faculties to minister in a parish have been revoked, priests who have "left ministry," but not through the proper channels, even priests who are guilty of sexual abuse and have been defrocked—all remain in need of the mercy of Christ, *all are hurting members of the Church*, all need our prayers that they can once again find their way, repent, recover the faith that has been lost, and like us, one day, by God's mercy, find salvation.

The Support of Friends

We priests know very well—because we've explained it to others, we've counseled people, we've spoken about it in homilies—that anyone, married, single, or celibate, at any age, will from time to time experience loneliness. But knowing this does not make us any less susceptible to the loneliness that can present itself in our lives.

Much has been written about the problem of loneliness in priestly life and the maladies that can arise from it. It's been the topic of multiple studies in recent decades and the frequent focus of reflections at priest retreats. It's led many to question the Church's requirement of celibacy, and so on.

I'm not going to belabor the point here. We know loneliness in priestly ministry is real, that it constitutes a problem afflicting many priests, and frankly accounts for much of what can go wrong in priestly life.

It goes without saying as well that one obvious antidote to loneliness is the art of healthy solitude: quiet and mental rest; prayer and contemplation; the enjoyment of "disconnecting" for a time from ministry and getting away; a regular day off, a good vacation, and an annual retreat; hitting the couch from time to time with a good book, or a good movie and a bowl of popcorn; a ball game, a night at the opera, a walk on the beach; hiking, biking, kayaking, skydiving—whatever.

Yet, in my personal experience, the key to beating loneliness in priestly life has always been friendships. And here I'm not referring to acquaintances that are normally superabundant in priestly ministry, or to the myriad good folks at the parish who smile, shake hands, and occasionally hug us on Sundays. Much less do I mean "friends" of the social media sort. I mean *friendship*: as in the deeply interpersonal, enduring, and emotionally fulfilling relationships that really merit the name. And in these I have been abundantly blessed—especially with laymen and women. I honestly don't know how I would persevere in my calling without them.

Priests don't need me to tell them about the value of friendships. We get it. We need them and want them. Yet, for any number of reasons personal friendships can remain elusive in priestly life.

For one thing, if friendships are to exist at all in a priest's life, they normally have to be found outside of the realm of his ministry. It goes without saying that the love, support, kindness, and esteem of parishioners for their priests—which hopefully they put on display in a hundred different ways—is vital for our perseverance in the ministry. But as wonderful and crucial as it is, it's still no substitute for friendships. In the parish or ministerial setting, the priest is inevitably in a position of leadership, guidance, and service, where the vulnerability and self-disclosure required for deep friendship would normally be inappropriate.

Genuine friendships with brother priests can also remain paradoxically a challenge. Because priests are so often ruggedly independent, vulnerability with a brother priest can be difficult. The much-heralded "priestly fraternity," where it can be had, will normally be infrequent; though enjoyable, it may often remain simply at the level of camaraderie, the swapping of stories, and good-natured banter—which is all well and good, but which can't of itself fulfill the need for emotional intimacy.

Priests, like any human being, need interpersonal communion; we just need it in a degree appropriate to our celibate state and within proper interpersonal boundaries. Appropriate emotional intimacy—not to be confused with emotional dependency—is part and parcel of human fulfillment and all-around well-being: to be vulnerable but without becoming emotionally needy, to communicate emotion with prudence and balance, and to share and receive appropriate gestures of affirmation and affection. Genuine friendships, and the emotional intimacy they provide, afford priests that profound sense of peace, stability, and security that fuels our capacity to serve the people of God.

Sustaining personal friendships is an art form, but it also boils down quite frankly to hard work. Because we priests are sometimes our own worst enemies, we might find ourselves unwilling to invest the time and energy that friendships require. And in the absence of such friendship, priests can then be tempted to fill the void with activity, with "ministry" or other substitutes. And that's where the problems can start.

Before suffering his passion, Jesus went to Bethany to enjoy, one last time, the intimacy of his friends Lazarus, Martha, and Mary; to share one last meal together (see Jn 12:1-3). I've always believed that in his humanity Jesus needed them—he *needed* his friends. So too, a priest needs his Bethany; he simply cannot genuinely thrive in a commitment to celibate chastity without at least a few close and emotionally intimate friendships. Such friendships are a gift from God. If they seem elusive, we need to wait patiently. God knows we need them. If we continue to knock, surely that door will eventually be opened to us. But when that door opens, we also have to be ready to do our part, and to put in the time and effort that our friends require and deserve.

Friends of Jesus and Ministers of the Mystery

As important as human friendships are, if we priests are going to avoid many potential pitfalls, we must rediscover again and again that our lives and ministry are ultimately anchored in our friendship with Jesus Christ. He called us. His friendship can vitalize us every day. He gave us this immense gift of being ministers of the mysteries of God (see 1 Cor 4:1). As often as we rediscover this truth, we are reminded that the priesthood is not a matter of doing and having, but a matter of *being*.

A future of vitality in the Catholic priesthood is possible if, on a daily basis, we plumb the depths of our being and rediscover that interior identification—*conformity*—with Christ we received the day of our ordination, and understand intimately, as the Second Vatican Council put it, that "the Mystery of Christ, which affects the whole course of human history, exercises an unceasing influence on the Church, and operates mainly though the ministry of the priest."[17] For if, in the words of Henri de Lubac, the Church's "whole end is to show us Christ, lead us to him, and communicate his grace to us," how much more so the priest? The priest exists, like the Church, "solely to put us into relation with [Christ]."[18]

Called to be ministers of the Mystery, we grope in our own humanity, in our temperament, limitations, and foibles. We are certainly needed in the Church—but we too have great needs, beginning with the love, support, friendship, and good *example* of our lay brothers and sisters. And when the Lord approaches us and offers us his cross, as we struggle to embrace it, that's the moment we need to reaffirm our "yes," our "Amen" to his "Come, follow me." As often as we can do that, aided by his grace, we have the opportunity to experience again the comfort, consolation, and joy of drinking deeply from the Mystery of Christ in us, and discovering our lives to be once again conformed to his cross.

CHAPTER 4

CƦ

When the Charity of Many Grows Cold

"I would suggest ... that all of you Christians, missionaries and all,
must begin to live more like Jesus Christ."

—Mahatma Gandhi

When Father Antonio Spadaro, SJ, editor in chief of the Italian journal *La Civiltà Cattolica*, asked Pope Francis in August 2013 what kind of Church he dreams of, the pontiff responded:

> [T]he thing the church needs most today is the ability to heal wounds and to warm the hearts of the faithful; it needs nearness, proximity. I see the church as a field hospital after battle. It is useless to ask a seriously injured person if he has high cholesterol and about the level of his blood sugars! You have to heal his wounds. Then we can talk about everything else. Heal the wounds, heal the wounds.

The image is powerful. Field hospitals in the midst of armed conflicts are places where heroic military doctors, nurses, and medics employ all their talents to save fallen soldiers. Life-threatening wounds must be attended to first. It's messy, bloody work: hands in the carnage, everyone all-in, trying to save every life that can be saved. And to Pope Francis' point: a medic's first concern in the field hospital is not whether his patient is overweight.

In one sense, the metaphorical field hospital of the Catholic Church is where all of us, laity and clergy alike, can encounter and care for a wounded world. We do so in our parishes and faith communities; in our charitable organizations, missions, and healthcare ministries; in thousands of "field hospitals" of the Church throughout the world. There we care for the homeless, the elderly, the dying, couples whose marriages are on the rocks, children from broken homes, the poorest of the poor, the addicted, victims of human trafficking—a wounded world.

But as the previous chapters have suggested, in addition to the wounded world the Church hopes to love and serve, we cannot ignore those within our own faith communities who are hurting. It seems this is what Pope Francis has in mind: "to heal wounds and to warm the hearts *of the faithful.*" And of these, I would suggest that, up front and center, we must attend to those whose wounds originated *from within the Church.*

If that is where we need to begin, then there are questions that require honest answers: Do we even know who the wounded members of our Catholic faith communities are? Do we care to know? And not for nothing, but how is the morale inside your local "field hospital"? What is the internal culture like? How do the ministers of mercy *treat each other*? In our parishes, chanceries and ministries, do we find toxic environments characterized by "hatreds, rivalry, jealousy, outbursts of fury, acts of selfishness, dissensions, and factions" that St. Paul deplored in some of his first Christian communities (see Gal 5:19-20)—or worse? How can the Church be a field hospital to serve the world's wounded while internally we slowly devour our own?

In previous chapters we have examined some of the deeper wounds borne by some of our brothers and sisters in the faith. We've also noted the resistance to acknowledge those hurts at the pastoral level. In this chapter, I want to reflect further on how

Catholics hurt in the Church today, on our attitudes toward those hurts, and on the virtue of charity and its place in our lives.

Peggy's Story

It is sad that a story like the following—we'll call the author Peggy—is all too typical. Here's how she describes what happened to her:

> It was nearly two years of hurt and fear. I am the secretary and the DRE at the parish, so my job relies on a good working relationship with the pastor. This pastor was past retirement age and had health issues. His homilies were part story/part stand-up comedy routine. He took liberties with the liturgy, particularly with the Creed (he would make up a "repeat after me" version). There were parishioners who loved him for that because faith came across as "anything goes" or [as] a joke.
>
> One day, while doing payroll, he was mad that I needed to call the chancery to make sure the withholding was right, and he left my office cursing and throwing his fist in the air. He actually left the building and drove around until after I left for home.
>
> One time a parishioner asked for contribution envelopes. He told me to wait until they asked again (seems he was aware they didn't have a lot of money). The second time they came to the office and asked for them he was present and told them that he was going to have to remind me again because "she can't remember anything." (I was standing four feet away and heard every word.) I honestly have no idea how many times he lied to parishioners about me.

He frequently told me that I never get anything right, and I mess up everything. I did mess stuff up because I was a nervous wreck. I was told that I wasn't even smart enough to answer the phone. I wasn't allowed to get the mail because I'd never be able to find the post office box.

God's hand was in every part of my getting this job. I knew that God felt my hurt, too. I had no idea what his plan was, but I had to trust. When the words and emotional hurt didn't go away, I documented everything. When, finally, I realized that I was being verbally and emotionally abused, I had to call the vicar general. Life was hell.

Eventually, I came to the realization that it wasn't about me. He would have been this way to whoever worked there at the time. It's a shame that a priest could hurt someone so deeply.

A saving grace was that I worked in a different town from where I lived. When I drove home, I would go to my local parish and spend some time in prayer with the Blessed Sacrament. I knew that the Eucharist was the very thing I needed to make it through. The more I hurt, the more I prayed. I knew that if I hung on to the hurt, I not only ran the risk of losing my faith, but it would affect my family's faith as well.

I also knew that I couldn't talk to many people about it. Many parishioners worshiped him. If I would have talked about what was going on, they would have glorified him and blamed me. I had four people I could talk to, and one was a priest. I went to confession often and appreciated the spiritual guidance I received there. I wanted to make sure my reactions, my thoughts, the temptation to gossip, the hurt, none of it would bring me down.

When the priest retired, I explained everything to the new pastor after a few days of getting acquainted. I needed to trust him, and as he'd already heard how terrible an employee I was (the previous pastor didn't mind gossiping and saying negative things about me to the new one), he needed to know the history. As it turns out, that was ultimately very helpful for healing.

I have always had, and still do have, great awe that God has allowed me to work so closely with his priests. Today I have a great love for the priesthood. I learned to trust in the Holy Spirit, to not hold on to hurt, to realize that this is the Body of Christ and that we must build it and not tear it down. Many times I've been reminded that through this experience, I was called to be the bigger Christian.

"That's Just the Way We Are." Really?

As I was writing this book, I would occasionally share a few details about its theme and scope. The most common reaction I received was something like: "Oh, *really*? Now, *that's* a book I want to read! That's a book that is *so* needed."

And sadly, it is. There are a lot of Peggys out there.

Now, a typical reaction to Peggy's story might be: "Listen, gal, you need to get a grip. Don't be so thin-skinned. These things are going to happen, and you just have to learn to suck it up."

Or another person might invite Peggy to "*offer* it up," as in spiritually uniting her sufferings to Our Lord's sufferings so that he might bring good from the whole situation.

Well, I am quite sure Peggy *did* in fact "offer it up."

But that does not solve our problem here.

A persistent and tragic flaw of Catholics throughout the centuries has been this relatively unquestioning acceptance of a certain status quo. It's the idea that Christians have *always* failed in charity, they always *will fail* in charity, and *nothing is going to change that.* "It's just the way we are."

Such an attitude constitutes an enormous problem for the Catholic Church today. By and large, we have settled for the status quo of a lethargic, anemic, indolent exercise of goodness and caring in our interpersonal relations with one another. We have grown accustomed to a life of charity grown cold. Granted, failures in charity are certainly not something new in the Church. But history cannot lead us simply to shrug our shoulders and say, "Oh, well." The fact that things have often more or less been this way in the Church *does not absolve us of the imperative of doing something to change the status quo.*

Yet there is something more perilous about our ecclesial context today in which these faults against charity occur. And it is simply this: today the spiritual moorings of many Catholics are more tenuous than ever. Unquestioned and rock-solid faith-based certainties, though not entirely a thing of the past, seem far more ephemeral in the contemporary mindset. Nothing is beyond question. Nothing is beyond scrutiny. Nothing is safe from the ravages of cynicism and our all too easily jaded spirits. Today it is easier than ever for a Catholic to lose faith and walk away from the Church because of a hurtful experience he or she has endured there.

Where's the Joy?

Here, I am going to go out on a limb—although a rather thick one, I believe—and make the following observation: in our day, far too many American Catholic parishes, rectories, chanceries, diocesan offices, and the like are simply not *joyful* places.

An overstatement?

Sadly, I think not.

These places can certainly often be pleasant, fun, and upbeat. I'm not suggesting they're places where kindness and goodness are altogether lacking. But I'm talking about *joy*—joy as in a fruit of the Holy Spirit, spontaneously emerging from hearts imbued with the good news about Jesus Christ. My experience in the Church tells me *this kind of joy* is sorely, sorely lacking.

If we're honest, the general mood in our places of worship and ministry is often much more like Ash Wednesday than Easter Sunday. The color of so many Catholic souls is gray, not gold. The general demeanor of so many Catholics, including many priests and bishops, often seems bereft of any glimmer of conviction that Jesus Christ has died and risen, that he is the Lord of our lives, that he has conquered sin and death, that he has opened up the way to eternal life—that he has *won the victory*.

Why is that?

Why do our Catholic communities, and especially our presbyterates, abound in so much negativity to begin with? Why can most bishops be described—as one bishop friend of mine aptly styled them—as "magnets for negativity"? Every dissatisfaction, disagreement, complaint, irritation, upset, frustration, demand, every cynical, snide, angry, nasty, snarky remark, it seems, makes its way to the bishop. Why is it, sadly, that such negativity is often the air we breathe?

Why is joy so often lacking in the life of the Church?

Here's a clue.

The *Catechism* describes joy as a fruit of charity, along with peace and mercy (see 1829). And, of course, as one of the twelve *fruits* of the Holy Spirit listed in Galatians 5:22-23, joy is listed second—after charity.

Genuine, supernatural, Holy Spirit-inspired joy is intimately related to charity. Where charity runs low, we should not expect to find joy. So here we have the explanation as to why our Catholic communities are so often joyless: because their members are so sorely lacking in charity, because we so frequently show ourselves to be loveless.

Of Charity and Charities

No doubt, you might be ready to object: the Catholic Church is the world's largest provider of charity, is it not? Few would dispute that. In the United States alone, Catholic Charities USA—with a multi-billion dollar annual budget and more than 2,500 local agencies serving 10 million people each year—ranks with United Way and the Salvation Army as one of America's leading providers of charitable social services. Add to that Catholic healthcare networks, St. Vincent de Paul societies, soup kitchens, food pantries, shelters, hospices, and innumerable charitable works conducted each day at the parish level.

No question: We excel at designing, running, and sustaining charities—*charitable works*—or what the Catholic tradition calls corporal works of mercy.

But here I will dare to ask a very uncomfortable question. In the internal, workaday culture of our charitable ministries, in our daily and mutual interactions with each other as co-laborers in the vineyard or the field hospital—whatever metaphor you prefer—is there *charity* as in fraternal benevolence, patience, kindness, and caring?

The obvious crucial distinction here is between charity as a corporal work of mercy (feeding the hungry, sheltering the homeless, clothing the naked, visiting the sick and imprisoned, and so forth) and the charity of 1 Corinthians 13.

Charity—in Greek, *agapē* (pronounced Ah-GAH-pay)—is the hallmark of Christianity. The emanation of genuine *agapē*-love from the first communities of Christian disciples marks something altogether new in human experience. *Agapē* love is the self-emptying love of Jesus:

Who, though he was in the form of God, did not regard equality with God something to be grasped. Rather, he emptied himself, taking the form of a slave, coming in human likeness; and found human in appearance, he humbled himself, becoming obedient to death, even death on a cross. (Philippians 2:6-8)

The best portrait of how Christ-like *agapē*-love actually looks when it is manifested in the life of the disciple of Jesus is found in St. Paul's timeless ode to that love:

Love is patient, love is kind. It is not jealous, [love] is not pompous, it is not inflated, it is not rude, it does not seek its own interests, it is not quick-tempered, it does not brood over injury, it does not rejoice over wrongdoing but rejoices with the truth. It bears all things, believes all things, hopes all things, endures all things. (1 Corinthians 13:4-7)

It's worth reflecting on those first two descriptive terms to try to articulate just what this novelty, this fruit of the Holy Spirit, translates into at the level of everyday life in the believer: *patience* and *kindness*. Paul lists these two characteristics together—and in that same order—among the fruits of the Holy Spirit in Galatians 5:22-23, and he also lists them, again together and in the same order, among the tools implemented by the apostles in the midst of the hardships they endure:

[T]hrough much endurance, in afflictions, hardships, constraints, beatings, imprisonments, riots, labors, vigils, fasts; by purity, knowledge, patience, kindness, in a holy spirit, in unfeigned love, in truthful speech, in the power of God. (2 Corinthians 6:4-7)

Kindness in particular deserves our careful attention. "Kindness" is the most common English translation of the Greek word *chrēstotēs*, which is how Paul uses it in Galatians 5:22. As such, the word appears only ten times in the Bible, only in the New Testament, and only in Paul's epistles (in slightly varying grammatical forms). Yet Paul's very deliberate use of the term is loaded with significance.

In Paul's mind, *chrēstotēs* is an essential character trait of the God of Israel, the Father of Jesus. In his epistle to the Romans, Paul depicts God's *chrēstotēs*, his loving-kindness, as aimed at eliciting the world's repentance (*metanoia*):

> Or do you hold his priceless kindness, forbearance, and patience in low esteem, unaware that the kindness of God would lead you to repentance? (2:4)

In Paul's mind, *chrēstotēs* is ultimately made most manifest in Christ Jesus, who, in turn, through lavishing the gifts of the Holy Spirit on the baptized, imbues his communities of disciples with *chrēstotēs* (Gal 5:22) as one of their chief distinguishing hallmarks and manifestations of genuineness. As the *Catechism* explains:

> He, then, gives us the "pledge" or "first fruits" of our inheritance: the very life of the Holy Trinity, which is to love as "God [has] loved us." This love (the "charity" of 1 Cor 13) is the source of the new life in Christ, made possible because we have received "power" from the Holy Spirit. By this power of the Spirit, God's children can bear much fruit.

> He who has grafted us onto the true vine will make us bear "the fruit of the Spirit: … love, joy, peace, patience, kindness, goodness, faithfulness, gentleness, self-control." (735-36)

Agapē love is all this—*chrēstotēs* and more. It is the love of Jesus present and active as a life-giving principle in the hearts of believers, a source of passionate goodness, of selfless concern for others. When this is lacking, when it has grown cold and fails to manifest itself in the internal life of the Church, what gets unleashed? A world of hurt and the stench of Catholic hypocrisy.

Internal Cultures of Hurt

No doubt, the Church is populated in part by individuals with genuinely problematic psychological issues: manipulators, narcissists, sociopaths, sexual predators. Some of these have historically made their way into seminaries, convents, religious orders, and diocesan priesthood. Others, living in the lay state, have in their own way found positions of influence, leadership, and control. And many have wreaked havoc.

They are one extreme.

Then there are the rest of us.

As human beings, we too—along with the narcissists and sociopaths—exist on a spectrum of mental health and interpersonal relational skill. While approximately 18 percent of Americans are enduring some form of diagnosable mental illness at any one time, anyone can be dealing with some degree of social dysfunctionality: foibles, interpersonal struggles, feelings of inferiority or superiority, jealousy, personal insecurities, fears, emotional neediness, and plain old selfishness.

To be sure, our default mode of human interaction is to *use others to satisfy our needs*. Such has been the human condition from the dawn of the species, and such remains our basic inclination even after baptism. While there may not be such a thing as a "selfish gene," our biology nonetheless appears to hard-wired us to look out for number one and to use others as means to achieve our ends.

With good reason did the philosopher Immanuel Kant arrive at a pristine insight into right moral action, valid as far as it goes, in the form of the principle that we are never to treat another person as a means to an end, but only as an end in himself. This, in fact, is how God treats us, for we are the only creatures God has willed for our own sake.[19]

Yet our all too common manner of dealing with each other in the Church, if we are bluntly honest, defaults back to our built-in selfishness, part of the residue of original sin that lingers even after baptism: we treat others as a means to an end.

This is the root that gives rise to so many weeds in the garden of virtue—impatience, ingratitude, callousness, indifference, insensitivity, and the list goes on. From these arise a plethora of hurts big and small. Such weeds pollute the internal cultures of our chanceries, ministerial offices, presbyterates, parishes, and rectories.

It is altogether too commonplace to discover pockets within our Catholic communities infested with animosities, nastiness, detraction, anger, and outright hatred—willfully consented to, or at least culpably tolerated; with intrigues and drama; with competitiveness, turf wars, and jealousies; and with that gossip Pope Francis has likened to a kind of emotional terrorism.

There is the hurt derived from years on end of dealing with a deep-down sense of being used, the awareness that, in the estimation of those who exercise leadership over me, I am simply a cog in the system, a solution to a problem, an answer that makes someone else's life easier. The hurt derived from such experiences is far more common and widespread—and often more painful—than we would care to imagine.

After years of often selfless service and dedication, no one should be served at the end of their tenure with a perfunctory and mechanical show of gratitude—a goodbye party conducted with all the pro-forma niceties, the cake, the card signed by all, perhaps even a wristwatch everyone's chipped in for, yet conducted with an air of obligation and superficiality. Of course, sometimes there's not even that. There's just a last day on the job, a parting handshake and, oh yes, a reminder to "please turn in your keys before you leave."

Such treatment is sadly far too prevalent in the Church. It can lead you to wonder: Does anyone *really* care? If, in the internal cultures of our Catholic communities and places of ministry and worship, there flourished a more genuine compassion for our brothers and sisters, such episodes would hardly be as commonplace as they are.

Heal the Wounds, Heal the Wounds

In the Gospel of Matthew, we read:

Then they will hand you over to persecution, and they will kill you. You will be hated by all nations because of my name. And then many will be led into sin; they will betray and hate one another. Many false prophets will arise and deceive many; and because of the increase of evildoing, the love of many will grow cold. But the one who perseveres to the end will be saved. (24:9-13)

In Matthew's presentation of the end times, external persecution breeds tensions within the Church; the outer wickedness takes hold among the brethren. Many, dismayed (literally, scandalized) by the persecution, will fall away. And many will "hate one another." They will betray one another. False prophets will arise. The depiction implies tensions, suspicions, and shrouds of confusion and uncertainty, all of which begin to tear at the fabric of peaceful and loving communion in the one faith. Malice will abound among brothers and sisters in Christ. And because of this overabundance of anger, betrayal, and hatred, the love, the Christian *agapē*, of many in the Church will grow cold—literally "will be blown cold" as by a chilling breeze.

Is Matthew's Gospel presenting us with the vision of the end times, or with a vision of a chapter in the Church's history that it has lived through hundreds of times over already throughout her two millennia of existence?

What we can say, almost as an inexorable law of Christian realism, is that where malice abounds among brothers and sisters in Christ, genuine Christian *agapē* love has grown cold and will continue to grow cold.

Our Church needs help.

Our parishes are populated by the walking wounded.

You might be one of them.

Hopefully the preceding chapters have afforded us the opportunity to confront this reality more personally. Before our communities of faith can really function as field hospitals for a hurting world beyond the Church, we have to acknowledge and attend to the wounded among us, beginning with those who have been hurt in their experience of the Catholic Church itself.

The answer, as hopefully will become evident in the chapters that follow, is what Pope Francis has called a "revolution of tenderness," a far-reaching, repentant, and passionate return to lives of intense and intentional *agapē* love—the love Jesus continues to teach his disciples, the love he wishes to instill and set ablaze in the heart of every human person.

CHAPTER 5

ↄ

Who Am I to Judge?

"It is true ... that mercy does not
exclude justice and truth,
but first and foremost we have to say
that mercy is the fullness of justice
and the most radiant manifestation
of God's truth."

—Pope Francis

Full disclosure: I disagree with those who say that the Church's teachings on contraception, cohabitation, divorce and remarriage, homosexuality, and so on, need to change. I happen to stand by those teachings.

But I also believe it's essential to *listen* to those who disagree. And I must admit that I've not always done a good job at that.

This book, and this chapter in particular, are the product of much listening I've done lately. But here, I am asking the reader, in turn, to please listen to me with an open mind. I hope this chapter can truly be a kind of dialogue—or at least a meaningful contribution to many dialogues it might provoke.

Early in his pontificate, Pope Francis responded to a question regarding homosexual persons. His response—on the face of it, ambiguous—drew an enormous amount of media attention. Many wondered if the Pontiff was signaling a change in the Church's teaching on homosexuality.*

The Pope responded: "Who am I to judge?" In a later publication, he had the opportunity to clarify what he meant:

On that occasion I said this: If a person is gay and seeks out the Lord and is willing, who am I to judge that person? I was paraphrasing by heart the *Catechism of the Catholic Church* where it says that these people should be treated with delicacy and not be marginalized. I am glad that we are talking about "homosexual people" because before all else comes the individual person, in his wholeness and

---

* An obligatory note on the terminology I use in this chapter to discuss this complex and difficult topic: I use "homosexual person" as synonymous with the phrase "person who experiences same-sex attraction." While I do not endorse self-identification by reference to one's sexual identity, "homosexual person" is a term used in Church documents as well as in the *Catechism*. It is also less awkward than the longer explanatory phrase. Those terms are to be distinguished from the terms lesbian, gay, bisexual, or transgender, and from their corresponding acronym, LGBT. For the sake of clarity and simplicity, I will use either the term "homosexual" or the phrase "person who experiences same-sex attraction" to refer to the broader population of persons who are same-sex attracted whether they adopt an actively homosexual lifestyle or not. I will use the term "gay" to mean persons (whether gay, lesbian, bisexual, or transgender) who *do* adopt that lifestyle or at least identify with elements of the broader LGBT culture—or "gay culture," as I might refer to it. Readers should keep in mind that not every person who experiences same-sex attraction embraces that lifestyle or identifies with gay culture. Some people live with the attraction and strive not to act on it out of religious and moral convictions. I use the term "LGBT community" to refer to that portion of the population who do in fact find a sense of community with others who have similar sexual orientations (whether they are sexually active themselves or endorse same-sex sexual activity or, on the contrary, strive to live celibate lifestyles). And I use the term "LGBT Catholics" to refer to those Catholics who likewise so identify and find a sense of community based on sexual orientation. My use of those terms does not signify my agreement with the manner in which these Catholic brothers and sisters choose to identify themselves.

dignity. And people should not be defined only by their sexual tendencies: Let us not forget that God loves all his creatures, and we are destined to receive his infinite love.[20]

I will return eventually in this chapter to the issue of homosexuality and the Catholic Church, undoubtedly one of the most contentious issues in the Church today. Pope Francis' words of clarification shed abundant light not only on that issue, but on a broader reality I first wish to address here.

Disagreement with the Church

Catholics who disagree with the Church's teaching on issues such as homosexuality, contraception, abortion, cohabitation before marriage, divorce and civil remarriage, and so on, can feel hurt by a Church that seemingly resists what they perceive to be reasonable calls for change—given the times we live in.

Far more commonly, however, it seems that Catholics actually *don't* experience emotional hurt over these issues. In fact, they would seem to live quite at peace in their disagreement with the Church's teaching, very likely because they have been taught (and now in good faith sincerely believe), that it is okay to disagree with the Church on those matters.

Many feel the Church's moral teaching is utterly out of touch with people in their real, day-to-day lives. Others feel that because of the Church's long history of unsavory scandals, and the hypocrisy of so many of its shepherds, the Church's moral authority has gone bust. For these and other reasons, American Catholics are generally of the mind that the Church should keep its nose out of everyone's proverbial bedroom. Yet there are Catholics who are internally conflicted over these issues: they know what the Church teaches, they believe that they *should be following* what the Church teaches, and nonetheless they speak and act to the contrary.

Tensions over the Church's moral teachings can become very personal when they revolve around some of the most intensely intimate realities we confront as human beings: the desire for sexual companionship, falling in love, marital fidelity, raising children, loving an actively gay child, sibling, or friend. Those tensions can, as well, take a severe toll on relationships and on religious practice, driving not a few baptized Catholics to part ways with the Church.

Is Silence on Moral Questions a Better Option for the Church Today?

Not only outside the Catholic Church but also within, people raise a red flag at the suggestion—in a homily, in the *Catechism*, in a conversation—that there are certain choices and behaviors which in and of themselves are morally problematic, especially in the realm of sexuality (at least as long as we're talking about consenting adults).

Both within and outside the Church there is a broad consensus among Americans that the Church's ministers, catechists, and teachers should just keep quiet on issues of human sexuality. The thought seems to be that religion, after all, is about *faith or one's creed*, not about *behavior* or "lifestyle choices."

Ne'er the twain shall meet?

Conformity to the cultural demand for acceptance, affirmation, and tolerance seems to require us to remain silent about the assessment of behavior—with the obvious exception of those behaviors that inflict some yet broadly accepted sense of harm, unfairness, or injustice on others.

So, if we dare express any negativity in regard to just about any specific behavior, much less describe it as "unnatural," "disordered," or "sinful," we are taken to be demeaning and condemnatory of the persons who might happen to engage in such behaviors. We are guilty of "judging" them.

"My Values" Versus the Church's Moral Teaching

We have become accustomed to understanding ourselves—Catholic or not—as our own moral compasses. We were instructed from kindergarten onward that choosing our own values was essential to becoming mature adults one day.

There's a grain of truth in there—but only a grain.

And even if people do look beyond themselves and their values to discover moral guideposts, there is less incentive than ever, it seems, to find such guideposts in the Church's teaching on moral issues. For many a Catholic, "what I believe" (creed) and "how I live my life" (behavior) have become disconnected in day-to-day living; it's been ingrained in us that morality, like religion, is a private matter. Consequently, we live in the era of the privatization of moral values and faith—two realms of our subjective experience that evolve and influence us independently one from the other, and both from the Church. At best, for most Catholics, what the Church teaches is considered one among several viable options to consider when, and if, they seek moral input in their lives.

This is all very strange because it is so contrary to the experience of the early Church. One of the earliest expressions used to refer to Christianity in the first century of its existence was "the Way" (Acts 9:2; 19:9,23). To live as a disciple of Jesus was a way of life, a life-changing, *behavior-altering* experience. "So whoever is in Christ is a new creation" (2 Cor 5:17).

The gift of faith brought about a profound change in the new believer: life, behavior, attitudes, outlook, comportment, sexual behavior—everything was affected:

> That is not how you learned Christ, assuming that you have heard of him and were taught in him, as truth is in Jesus, that you should put away the old self of your former way of life, corrupted through deceitful desires, and be re-

newed in the spirit of your minds, and put on the new
self, created in God's way in righteousness and holiness of
truth. (Ephesians 4:20-24)[21]

In the early Church, newly baptized Christians would look to
the Christian community—and particularly to those given the authority to teach about this new way of life, namely, the apostles
(their oral and written instructions to the communities) and the
bishops and presbyters appointed by them—to learn how to live
this "Way," how to conform their behavior, even their personal sexual behavior, to what was becoming of this "new creation," the new
man or woman in Christ.

This is why Paul tells the first communities of Christians
founded by him to imitate what they have seen in his own comportment: "Keep on doing what you have learned and received and
heard and seen in me. Then the God of peace will be with you"
(Phil 4:9); "Be imitators of me, as I am of Christ" (1 Cor 11:1).

In other words, from the very dawn of Christianity, faith in
Jesus and one's own personal behavior were intimately connected.
The early Church knew nothing of a private realm of personal morality and lifestyle choices that were disconnected from the faith
one professed and the Church's moral guidance.

The Church has always understood that the moral life is where
we live out our faith, where professed creed becomes lived behavior—in the personal moral choices we make every day, including
choices with regard to our sexuality. We have, through the centuries, been challenged by the conviction that *we ourselves are not
the origin and source* of the moral values by which to live our lives.
Christ and his moral teaching, entrusted to the Church, are that
origin and source.

Reticence to embrace the Church's teaching can indicate a
rather shallow and misshapen understanding of how Catholics are
expected to live their faith. Being Catholic ultimately is *not* simply
about rule-following. If a Catholic believes he or she can take or

leave the Church's moral teaching on X, Y, or Z, it's often because deep down that person understands those "rules" to be little more than a set of policies that can be changed with time, disagreed with, or declined in favor of other moral policies that seem more appealing—for instance, those offered by contemporary culture.

I invite Catholics who disagree with the Church's teaching on hot-button moral issues to look at this body of teaching not as a matter of rules or policies but as guideposts to living a genuinely fulfilling human life. Being Catholic is not about following rules; it's about following Jesus, who came that we "might have life and have it more abundantly" (Jn 10:10). If there is a teaching to be followed, it only makes sense when embraced out of fidelity to Christ and by trusting that his teaching has been transmitted to us in and through the Church, and this teaching will not fail us.

I challenge my brothers and sisters to ask themselves whether—in spite of all the many arguments to the contrary—there is not still wisdom to be found in the Church's moral teaching, and to ask whether, through these teachings, the Holy Spirit could not be guiding us "to all truth" (Jn 16:13). Could these teachings, and the wisdom they contain, actually be guideposts directing us toward genuine human fulfillment and true happiness?

Judgmentalness Versus Moral Judgment

When people take offense at the notion of judging someone, they usually mean that by judging, one is rendering a condemnatory assessment about a person. That's judgmentalness, and it's problematic. Such judgments are so often unfair, unfounded, and mistaken. With good reason we should normally question an initial negative impression we might have of another person. And undoubtedly much harm is done, especially in the life of the Church, when we allow judgmentalness to run amok.

To be sure, we are never in a position to know, to possess a certain and comprehensive knowledge of the internal state of conscience of another person—what a person truly holds in their heart, or their actual degree of moral responsibility for their choices and actions. In this sense, only God is truly the judge.[22]

But of course we understand that at times we have no choice but to *assess someone's intentions or character* as indicated by their actions, albeit within the limitations of our human capacity. Police officers, for example, must often make rapid-fire judgments about individuals when first arriving at the scene of a disturbance: Is the person now addressing me cogent, truthful, agitated, hiding something, incoherent?

Parents, with good reason, assess the character of their children's playmates and of the kids their teens wish to date. I am not being judgmental when I discover that a friend has been cheating on his wife for years and I call him on it.

In the confessional, it is the priest's obligation to try to arrive at some assessment of the penitent's spiritual and moral health: Has this person—based on what is being confessed—likely been guilty of mortal sin? Is this person genuinely repentant? Is there some element—immaturity, ignorance, fear—that might have diminished his or her degree of moral responsibility?

Authentic charity does not preclude the rendering of such judgments—properly understood within their limits. In fact, at times it requires us to make them. Nor is our arriving at such judgments necessarily to commit the fault of being judgmental. The upshot, however, is that rendering and communicating judgments of this nature might be unavoidably hurtful to the recipient.

Person and Behavior

But the crucial point, it seems to me, and the crux of many tensions and hurts, is our inability at times to distinguish between *behav-*

ior and *person*. Obviously, the two concepts are intimately related; but there is nonetheless an important way we need to distinguish them.

Surely a mother who angrily objects to her daughter's decision to drop out of college to pursue a career as a tattoo artist (behavior) can still be understood as loving her daughter (person). In fact, many would understand that the intensity of her objections is driven precisely by the intensity of her love for her daughter. There is no reason to conclude that because she objects to her daughter's values and lifestyle choices, she, therefore, thinks her daughter is a bad person.

My point is that the negative judgment—even of another's character—need not constitute a rejection or condemnation of the person. It need not be interpreted as unloving. While such judgments are not infrequently thoughtless or premature or based on bias, prejudice, personal animus, or what have you, they can also be an occasion for introspection, for a reexamination of one's values, for dialogue, or repentance, or reconciliation between persons, or even for a change of lifestyle. The prudent rendering of such honest judgments about others, motivated by concern for the genuine good of the individual, need not be a problem.

Of course, no one likes being on the receiving end of another's assessment that "You are making some really bad choices" or "You can never fulfill yourself that way." And while it's hard enough receiving that from a parent, a spouse, or a best friend, what happens when those assessments seem to emanate from the Church?

I happen to believe very strongly, for example, in consonance with the Church's understanding of the gift of human sexuality and its connection to our ultimate happiness, that persons who engage in same-sex sexual acts, who undergo surgery in an attempt to alter their biological sexual identity, and so on, are in fact making really bad choices, hurting themselves, and jeopardizing their own human fulfillment.[23]

If some believe that by embracing such tenets or expressing them in writing I am engaging in "hate speech" or further "marginalizing" LGBT individuals, well, all I can say is that we likely have very different conceptions of morality (and perhaps even of reality itself in many ways), or at the very least—like the mother and daughter above—we have fundamentally different values. But does my unwillingness to validate their lifestyle choices mean we can't love each other anyway? Does that mean that the love I could have for them is a farce and a contradiction in terms?

The Church and Persons Who Experience Same-Sex Attraction

According to a 2015 Gallup poll, 3.8 percent of Americans identify themselves as lesbian, gay, bisexual, or transgender. The same poll indicated that more than a third of Americans (33 percent of those polled) estimate that more than 25 percent of the American population identifies as LGBT. More than a third of Americans overestimate the reality by at least 20 percent.[24]

Yet 3.8 percent of the American population these days means roughly between twelve and thirteen million people. That is not insignificant (the Asian population in the United States in 2015 was estimated at just over eighteen million).

A 2014 Pew Research study indicated that 57 percent of Catholics favor allowing gay and lesbian couples to legally wed, and fully 85 percent of self-identified Catholics ages 18-29 said that homosexuality "should be accepted by society."[25] I am inclined to believe, based on figures such as these and other experiences, that a majority or near majority of American Catholics do not have a moral objection to the idea of same-sex sexual activity.

Yet we Catholics are members of a Church which still claims to hold to the following convictions: that it is God's plan that sexual intercourse occur only within marriage between a man and a woman; that every act of intercourse be open to the possible creation of human life if the spouses are of childbearing age; that sexual acts between persons of the same sex cannot fulfill these two conditions and are therefore incapable of contributing to genuine human flourishing, and so on. Again, one could infer that a large percentage of American Catholics, likely a majority, simply do not believe or hold to these moral convictions.

What are we to make of all this?

I want to think that the vast majority of Catholic priests, in contrast, still embrace these convictions. But how those convictions spill over into lived pastoral practice with gay parishioners is another question altogether. It's safe to say there is a range of approaches. I suspect many adopt something of a don't-ask-don't-tell policy. For parishioners who openly identify as gay, who actively engage in a gay lifestyle, who live with a gay partner and go to Church with that partner, most priests try to be as welcoming as they can be. Most would (correctly in my opinion) refrain from inviting these individuals into pastoral and ministerial roles within their parishes. But most do baptize these couples' children. They greet them cheerfully when they come to pick up their kids from religious education class. They take pictures with the couples and their kids after first Communions. They may even share a meal with them in their homes.

Yet no matter how kind, open, and inviting I am as a priest to these brothers and sisters of mine, no matter how "welcoming," how many times I smile, shake hands, greet, and so on, the fact that I hold to such convictions is intolerable for the vast majority of persons who identify as LGBT and, in their minds, antithetical to affirming their human dignity. They believe that someone who fails to affirm that same-sex love is of equal dignity as heterosexual love (as I fail to affirm it) or who holds that acting on same-sex attraction is immoral (as I hold it to be), cannot at the same time be "accepting of" LGBT individuals. In their view, by insisting on and clinging to principles such as these I will always be considering them second-class human beings, and my supposed love and acceptance will be a sham. It's that simple.

Or is it?

I worked on this chapter in the summer of 2016, in the wake of the Orlando, Florida, shooting massacre that took forty-nine lives and which was arguably perpetrated at least in part out of hatred for the LGBT community. In the public discussion that followed this tragedy, the question of the moral culpability—not to say complicity—of conservative Christians and their views on homosexuality was raised and explored with unprecedented directness. Most notably, one *New York Times* op-ed even invited Christians "to repent for the ways they've helped create a culture that devalues L.G.B.T. people." Only a few weeks later, Cardinal Reinhard Marx of Freising, Germany, stated very publicly his belief that "as church and as society we have to say sorry [to homosexuals]." When questioned days later about the comment in an interview with reporters, Pope Francis affirmed the cardinal's comment while putting it in a broader context of many other things for which Christians should seek forgiveness, especially for social sins of omission.[26]

I have no doubt that across the globe Catholics have much to apologize for in their treatment of LGBT individuals, where they have failed to genuinely accept them as persons or treat them with respect, compassion, and sensitivity—as should be our approach according to the *Catechism of the Catholic Church*. The one thing Catholics cannot apologize for is the Church's consistent teaching about God's plan for marriage and human sexuality. Yet some persons, who of late are requiring "repentance," seem to be requiring just that. I take it that repentance here entails—ultimately—setting aside our core convictions about human sexuality and marriage altogether.

So, we find ourselves at a seemingly insurmountable impasse: actively lesbian, gay, bisexual, or transgender individuals think they will never *ever* feel fully accepted or loved by people like me who maintain the kind of convictions I maintain about same-sex attraction and how to deal with it in a morally acceptable way.

That's a hard place to be in; it's hard for all of us.

Nonetheless, we are called to love each other even in the midst of moral tensions. Yet, to love one another in the Church today does not require us to avoid discussion of moral issues. Genuine *agapē* love does not preclude our commitment to moral principles on which we might strongly, even vehemently, disagree. On the contrary, it invites us to a profound dialogue on these issues. The best response to our present circumstances is more dialogue, *not less*; not to remain respectfully silent, but to engage in a robust discussion of these questions in the public square: What is the nature of marriage? Can contraceptive sex have a harmful effect on marital love? What is gender and gender identity? What is erotic love? What is friendship? What does sex have to do with it? A church that remains silent on these questions is a church that is profoundly failing its mission to humanity.

There would be a lot less pain resulting from these issues in the experience of Catholics who say they disagree with Church teaching if we could attempt to tone down our emotional response to them and get back to civil discourse by actively listening to one another, and by carefully reasoning about these issues. Silence won't get us there.

To my brothers and sisters who experience same-sex attraction, I owe you my honesty. I owe the truth of what I believe as a disciple of Jesus and what I believe are fundamental truths about human life, love, sexuality, and fulfillment that God has revealed to us through his Word.

But I also owe you my sensitivity to your struggles. It must be painful for homosexual persons, and in particular for those who strive to embrace the Church's teaching on homosexuality to hear their sexual orientation described in the *Catechism* as something "objectively disordered":

The number of men and women who have deep-seated homosexual tendencies is not negligible. This inclination, which is objectively disordered, constitutes for most of them a trial. They must be accepted with respect, compassion, and sensitivity. Every sign of unjust discrimination in their regard should be avoided. These persons are called to fulfill God's will in their lives and, if they are Christians, to unite to the sacrifice of the Lord's Cross the difficulties they may encounter from their condition. (2358)

What it affirms about respect and compassion is good—but it does not lessen the sting of the preceding line.

I have utter admiration and respect for Catholic men and women who live with same-sex attraction while striving to embrace the Church's teaching on sexuality. I have been humbled to accompany several on at least part of their life's journey. These are men and women who have grappled with a Gordian knot of questions about themselves and their orientation; they've wrestled with God and with what he allowed in their lives—a unique mystery of personal existence and fidelity to Christ which, many times over, they have united to the sacrifice of the Lord's cross.

I do not believe that holding to the Church's teaching on sexuality is incompatible with offering LGBT individuals sincere friendship and companionship, nor with making them feel welcome and wanted in our parishes. I hope actually to know them *not* as defined by their sexual orientation—but simply as the *persons* they are.

Which leads to a question: Do LGBT Catholics have particular gifts and qualities to offer their Christian communities? Of course they do—but I make that affirmation with one rather significant qualifier: they have gifts and qualities to offer, not in virtue of being lesbian, gay, bisexual, or transsexual, but in virtue of *being human persons.* And I again think especially of that small, yet significant number of same-sex-attracted Christians who are trying to live *celibate lifestyles* in accord with biblical teaching on same-sex sexual activity. They deserve our respect, support, and, especially, *our attention*. We need to listen to them tell their stories as they explore what it means to follow Jesus and share their particular personal gifts with the world and with the Church.[27]

As important as it is to *feel* welcomed, affirmed, and wanted, and to sense that one's gifts and talents are being appreciated and utilized, such a *feeling* is not what membership in the Catholic Church is about. Being a baptized Catholic is about following Jesus. It's about being a disciple. Can Catholics who experience same-sex attraction or gender dysphoria be disciples of Jesus? Of course they can. But the same challenges and exigencies apply to all of us—including biblical teaching on human sexuality and marriage.

❃

Although our disagreements on moral matters may be interminable, although Catholics will continue to struggle within themselves over the Church's teaching on human sexuality, the answer is not to abandon the Church, but to continue to grapple with these issues, thinking about them, praying about them, engaging in respectful dialogue with each other and in the public square, searching for the truth of the matter, and trying to understand well, and in depth, the Church's *reasons* for teaching what she does.[28]

I think, too, of that other kind of suffering endured within the Church due to the fact that so many Catholics live in habitual rejection of the Church's moral teaching on key issues. It's a kind of hurt experienced by the Mystical Body as a whole. It is certainly never recommendable to one's mental health to persist in a state of interior inconsistency, pitting what we say and what we do against what we actually believe to be the moral truth of the matter. And it certainly can't be good for the universal Church when millions of her members are unarguably living in contradiction to her moral teachings.

When all this causes us to hurt, we need to bring those hurts to Jesus. We need to continue to seek answers there, with the hope and serenity instilled in us by the truth that God loves each and every human person with infinite love, and that he invites each one of us to follow his Son Jesus through the "narrow gate," to "take up our cross," to form our consciences according to his Son's teaching, and then follow our consciences in our everyday choices.

Part II
Toward Personal Healing

CHAPTER 6

ભ

First Steps

"Too often we underestimate the power of a touch, a smile, a kind word, a listening ear, an honest compliment, or the smallest act of caring, all of which have the potential to turn a life around."

—Leo Buscaglia

In the very first days of my crisis, I was reminded of how flight attendants explain the proper use of the oxygen mask during their preflight safety instructions: they always tell you to adjust your own oxygen mask first before assisting others. I had already spent hours reaching out to others who had been devastated by the Legion crisis—phone calls, e-mails, counseling, trying to comfort and shed light. At night, there was only fitful sleep at best. I was really struggling emotionally and was fearful of what was happening to me. After a few days, it became very clear that I had no choice but to switch focus and do something to take care of *myself*. I had to adjust my own oxygen mask, and do it fast. I just didn't know exactly what to do. Fortunately, I had a friend who did.

Accepting Help

Sensing that I was emotionally shattered, she reached out and offered to fly me down to Louisiana for a week or two, and have me hunker down at her parents' house where I could decompress, recover some strength, and begin to process what had just happened to me. Although I could have come up with any number of excuses to turn down the offer, her gesture was so overflowing with understanding, love, and compassion—and my own mental state so worrisome—that I immediately accepted.

I cannot stress enough how crucial that step was: *to accept an offer of help.* That step was life-altering, and marked the beginning of my healing process.

As it turns out, my friend and her family were Hurricane Katrina survivors.

Little did I know that Nell and Guy—my friend's parents— would quickly become not only fast friends, but also my first mentors in how to deal with emotional trauma. And they knew *a lot* about dealing with emotional trauma.

Over the days, soothed and comforted by their incomparable Louisiana hospitality—*and* their out-of-this-world Cajun-Sicilian home cooking—I shared my story with them. And then in the days that followed, they began to share with me, little by little, their story—a story of survival. Not quite four years had passed since the tragic days of late August 2005, and talking about Katrina easily reopened wounds. If they were talking about it, they were telling me their story *for me—for my sake.*

In the immediate aftermath of Hurricane Katrina—the most destructive storm in U.S. history—the media focused heavily on New Orleans. But many other communities were as devastated as the Big Easy. Slidell—home to my friends Guy and Nell—was one such community. Located approximately thirty-four miles northeast of New Orleans, Slidell is nestled on the north shore of massive Lake Pontchartrain. Though technically not a lake, rather an estuary connected to the Gulf of Mexico, Pontchartrain is a 630-square-mile oval expanse of water with an average depth of twelve to fourteen feet. It was this enormous body of water that eventually wreaked much of the havoc endured by the communities of southern Louisiana. Multiple storm surges off the lake left a trail of devastation in their path.

Guy and Nell had raised their family in a moderately affluent canalled waterfront neighborhood. While their home of twenty-plus years was not obliterated by Katrina, it was severely damaged by the driving winds, storm surge, and eventual deposit of four feet of water, silt, sludge, and debris. If they wanted to keep their home, they would have to gut it down to a shell and rebuild.

Their choice to remain and rebuild was a critical turning point, but it came at a heavy cost. To the unspeakable heartbreak of losing home, furniture, valuables, mementos, pictures, keepsakes—so many of the heart's treasures—was added the nightmare of enduring the rebuilding effort: the Herculean task that lay before them of clearing, cleaning, and gutting the house; the lack of bare necessities; the waiting in line; the phone calls and being put on hold; the dysfunctionality of government agencies utterly unprepared to handle the devastation; the waiting for federal assistance; the constant uncertainty, frustration, and gut-wrenching sadness that gnawed away at them continually day after day.

Over time, they, like many Katrina survivors, developed symptoms of post-traumatic stress disorder. And not surprisingly. It seems this is just how the human psyche responds when we've lost so much, when our entire life has been turned upside down in a single day.

I will always remember one afternoon in the car with Guy as we were again sharing about their survival and my own recent personal catastrophe, and how he gently helped me to understand that what I had been through was like "a spiritual Katrina."

And while in many ways I felt uncomfortable drawing such a close comparison between my suffering and theirs—which seemed to me in so many ways incomparably worse—Guy and Nell insisted that the analogy fit, and as I listened to them, I began to get a sense of how I could recover—just as they had.

Their approach to healing was somewhat hit or miss. They re-counted how they reached out to friends and neighbors who were also rebuilding and formed a kind of support group. They remi-nisced how, every day, neighbors deliberately tried to share some piece of good news with each other—*anything* positive to keep spir-its up. One neighbor's breakthrough or success heartened everyone else. The venting of tensions and pent-up emotions was also vital.

Of course, faith was the heart of it all. Guy and Nell are deeply committed Catholics. When I asked Guy once to articulate what it took—on the human level—to stay, rebuild, and begin again, he spoke of three things.

He spoke of hope: the unshakable conviction that they were going to get through this. He also spoke of acceptance. Not unlike that pivotal milestone in the stages of grief, this meant getting to that place where he and Nell could accept that certain things were now gone, and gone forever, while acknowledging the new reality and taking hold of it.

But Guy also spoke—after a long pause to try to articulate pre-cisely what he meant—of what he called "conditioning." By this he meant the gradual awareness, as they strove day in and day out to put one foot in front of the other, that God had been preparing them throughout their lives for this moment. "He knows what's coming, even though we do not," he told me. "And God enables you … to just get it together."

That's a good metaphor for the healing process: God enabling you to "get it together" again. But if healing is a process of getting whole again, then other human beings—with whom we dare to be vulnerable and share our pain—are the glue.

Guidance, Support—and a Shoulder to Cry on

When you've suffered an emotionally traumatic event, you might be tempted to consider the hurt insignificant when compared with the sufferings of others. We might think that we are "making a mountain out of a mole hill" and that we should just get over it!

Granted, with many things that happen to us in life, there can be some merit to that approach. The best treatment for a bad case of hurt feelings sometimes is to put the issue in a broader context, step away from the barrage of emotions, and ask whether the real culprit here is not *me*—my misplaced expectations, my oversensitivity, my lack of a healthy sense of humor, taking myself too seriously, and the list could go on. That indeed might go a long way toward helping me get over it.

Quite another thing is genuine emotional trauma. Here we're truly dealing with a laceration of the spirit, an assault on the heart. Here we need to stop comparing ourselves with others, silence the inner voice that says we are exaggerating, and actually admit the hurt, recognize it, and validate it. Particularly, if our hurt occurred in the context of the Church and has brought us to the brink of questioning our faith, then this *is* a big deal. We should not let anyone convince us otherwise.

In addition to our minimizing what's happened to us, other obstacles can inhibit us from accepting help when it is offered to us, or from reaching out for it ourselves. As my friends Art and Laraine Bennett explain:

> Our pride ("I can do it myself"), our vanity ("I don't want to let people know how hurt I am"), or our laziness ("I do not have the time, energy, or money to get help") may prevent us from addressing the issue. There is also the issue of trust. This is often the most difficult barrier: I trusted before, and my trust was abused. How can I trust anyone again?
>
> Traumatic wounds are serious and generally need both spiritual guidance from a qualified priest, deacon, sister, or lay spiritual director and professional help from a qualified therapist. The integration of a spiritual and psychological healing is the best way to address these serious wounds.[29]

As Art and Laraine emphasize, addressing emotional trauma will often require a professional counselor or therapist. I was fortunate to be friends with the Bennetts. Art is a licensed marriage and family counselor with years of experience. I eventually reached out to him to get some coaching on how to deal with the array and vehemence of the emotions that I was experiencing. His help was invaluable. Likewise, I was blessed—as I've already shared earlier—to have the guidance of a very experienced spiritual director endowed with the gifts of discernment and prudence.

But as Art and Laraine rightly point out, there is also an issue of trust here, and of vulnerability. Opening up our hurt to another involves a risk. Being vulnerable means exposing the hurt. It means talking about it. And it means at times opening up the floodgates in a caring person's protective presence, and letting out emotions and, quite possibly, copious tears.

Sound spiritual guidance and, depending on the severity of the emotional trauma, therapy or counseling—these are key to the healing process, along with friends to lean on, and at least one shoulder to cry on. For some people, these are not easy to come by. And that can add to the heartache. But I'm a firm believer that where there's a will—and we have no reason to doubt that God wants our healing—there's a way. Sooner or later, experience tells me, the necessary connections can almost always be made, and we can find the right individuals to help us. It depends on God's mercy and guidance, of course, but it also depends on our willingness and determination to reach out, and not stop until we get the help we need.

Owning the Hurt

I began writing this book to help myself heal. That *I needed to heal* was a tough concept to swallow, though. I was a priest. I was in the business of ministering to others. *They* were the ones who needed healing. *Not me.* I consequently found myself, several months after my crisis had hit, reassuring friends that I was—in so many words—over it.

Thanks be to God, another close friend knew better. She herself had been through personal trauma of a kind that required years of healing. One evening at dinner with her and her husband, I was again making the case that I was doing much better, that I had healed, and that the hurt was behind me now. Having held her tongue patiently on previous occasions when I had made similar affirmations, this night she finally broke her silence, looked me in the eye, and laid down the hard truth: "Tom, you are *not* over this! Healing from a wound like yours is going to take a *long* time!"

This was tough stuff to absorb for someone who is in the business of helping others heal. I had not wanted to hear it—*but how I needed to hear it!* I had needed someone to force me to look directly into the gaping hole in the center of my being. She forced me to deal with reality: I was deeply wounded, and I was only at the *very beginning* of my healing process.

My friend's blunt honesty also helped me to start absorbing another reality: the wound was going to have a lasting impact on me. Sure enough, it wasn't going to define who I was (unless I let it), but neither was it just going away. Rather, the wound *and how I chose to deal with it* would have a lasting influence on who I would become from that point on in my life.

And this kind of ruggedly honest grappling with hard truths also left me wide open to God's light, to his grace and his healing touch. But it required me to accept and own those hard truths. God had made me a priest, and healer, and minister to others. But I had to absorb and embrace the reality that I was now very much a "wounded healer." Never in my life could I have imagined that this metaphor—brought into vogue by the spiritual writer Father Henri Nouwen in the 1970s—would come to characterize *me* so painfully well.

My friend's blunt honesty had provoked in me a kind of surrender. I was forced to put down my defenses. The painful experience of such negative emotions had led me to present to the outer world a kind of false self: a self that had gotten over it and had it all together again. It was a kind of denial. Now I was forced to stop deflecting the reality.

Most important, I was finally in a position to really bring my wounds to prayer.

Little by little, I started to understand that my wounds, as humiliating, embarrassing, and infuriating as they were, would not destroy me. My identity would not crumble and deteriorate because of what had happened. On the contrary, the hurt would ultimately enhance who I was. The hurt would not destroy me, it would not absorb me. Rather, *I would have to absorb it*, and this meant accepting what had happened and integrating it into my self-understanding. It meant owning the hurt.

And this, it seems to me, is a critical step in the healing process—most especially when wounds are life-altering: this happened to me; it is now part of who I am and will contribute to shaping who I become. And that's okay. And, in fact, I can now become a better person because of it.

Reaffirming Foundations

One of the effects of suffering a severe emotional trauma such as betrayal is the sense that our life has been upended. Our compass seems suddenly to fail, and we lose our north. Long-held convictions about life, love, and purpose—once foundational for our own self-understanding—can be abruptly shattered. It can give us the terrifying sensation of being held to the precipice of an existential void. Anxiety attacks and depression are not uncommon responses to such interior turmoil.

For many who have suffered wounds in the Church that shake their faith down to its very roots, the road to healing will require a return to, and a rediscovery of, the basic tenets of our faith contained in the Creed. With some hurts, the trauma can penetrate so deeply that a veritable re-anchoring of ourselves in the truths of revelation becomes essential.

Once I was able to accept how serious my wounds were, there came a time when, finally, I felt their full intensity. It's an inevitable part of the healing process. In my case, as I began to plumb the depths of my wounds, I found myself immersed in a spiritual desolation that lasted for several weeks. Everything seemed open to question: How many lies had I been subjected to? How had I ended up in this dysfunctional religious community in the first place? How had the Church failed to discover Maciel's deceptions? If so much of what I had believed in as a member of this community turned out to be lies, if the whole life project I had pursued for over twenty years was now obliterated, *what then was left*? What was true? What remained of my foundation?

On the inside, I was experiencing a kind of spiritual numbness. In my ministry, I often felt as if I were just going through the motions. Liturgy left me feeling empty. My preaching felt strained and unnatural. But worse, I felt a loss of affection for the Church. So many of her inner workings seemed so maddeningly dysfunctional at times. But I also began to experience the desolation of feeling that it was the Church that had hurt me, the Church that had failed to protect me. In revulsion, at times I experienced an almost irresistible urge to just run away: *I'm done! I'm outta here! I don't need this!*

And then it finally hit me: I was actually thinking of leaving the priesthood. I was actually toying with the possibility. Sure, I was a priest. I didn't doubt my calling. But was the catastrophe I had suffered too much? The pain too strong? Was I just too damaged to continue? That was my darkest moment.

When we're in the midst of the darkness, that's when we need to beg God to send us his light. Life has taught me that God never refuses *that* prayer. It's just a matter of not panicking, not giving in to despair. We have to ask humbly and then wait—patiently, confidently, and attentively.

And sure enough, there came, in the midst of my most intense struggle, a sudden insight, a moment of grace and light. And the clouds began to disperse.

Faced with the erosion of meaning in my life, it occurred to me that I had to go deep inside and find terra firma, I had to get down to the foundations of my own life and existence: What is immovable? What is certain? *What do I believe?*

I secluded myself in a private spiritual retreat precisely to search out these core truths of my life, in the presence of God, trying to let him guide and enlighten me. With his grace, I was able to take up once again that age-old invitation of St. Augustine: "Do not venture outwardly; enter rather into yourself; for in the interior of a man, truth is found." I had to rediscover from the inside who God had created and called me to be. This time away with God became a journey into my core beliefs: all the way down to the Creed, to the Incarnation, to Revelation itself.

My starting point was the acute awareness that no matter what had happened with my religious congregation, I had, in fact, eleven years earlier, been validly ordained a Catholic priest. Yet even for this fact there had to be a foundation, a deeper core of truths.

It was in a passage from Paul's Letter to the Ephesians that I found the answer I was looking for:

> For this reason I kneel before the Father, from whom every family in heaven and on earth is named, that he may grant you in accord with the riches of his glory to be strengthened with power through his Spirit in the inner self, and that Christ may dwell in your hearts through faith; that you, rooted and grounded in love, may have strength to comprehend with all the holy ones what is the breadth and length and height and depth, and to know the love of Christ that surpasses knowledge, so that you may be filled with all the fullness of God.

Now to him who is able to accomplish far more than all we ask or imagine, by the power at work within us, to him be glory in the church and in Christ Jesus to all generations, forever and ever. Amen. (3:14-21)

"Rooted and grounded in love." This line of sacred Scripture became for me a source of immense healing. The Maciel affair will remain one of the darkest chapters in the Church's recent history. Yet, it became clear to me that none of that, nor anything I had suffered, could destroy, minimize, or even touch the reality of the love of Jesus Christ. I was *rooted and grounded in love*, in the love of Jesus for me, and in my love for him. No hurt could take that away from me. No nightmare, no betrayal, no scandal could touch the love that Jesus and I shared. I rediscovered that, at my core, my life was anchored in that experience of the love of Jesus, something I was blessed to have experienced from an early age.

"Rooted and grounded in love" has come to mean for me that I am, at my very core, a human person, created and saved through the Word of God, loved by God from all eternity, and called to an eternal destiny. It means I am called to be a disciple of Jesus, to live the days of my life immersed in the mystery of Christ in us, "the hope for glory" (Col 1:27).

Where the wounds have threatened the very foundations of our faith and belief, the road to healing must lead us back eventually to what grounds us as Christians. No hurt, no matter how severe, can touch the love, the personal knowledge, the pledge of friendship stretching into eternity that Jesus offers us. To rediscover that we are anchored in Jesus, that "neither death, nor life, nor angels, nor principalities, nor present things, nor future things, nor powers, nor height, nor depth, nor any other creature will be able to separate us from the love of God in Christ Jesus our Lord" (Rom 8:38-39)—this is key to healing. Jesus is the reason why, ultimately, no matter how deep the hurt, *healing is always possible.*

CHAPTER 7

ॐ

Forgiving

"To forgive is to set a prisoner free and discover that the prisoner was you."

—Lewis B. Smedes

Sooner or later when we've been hurt, most of us get to a point where, if we're honest, we *want* to forgive, but maybe we just feel it's beyond our strength. That might not be the impression we give on the outside; we might still sound and feel very angry. Inside, however, we might sense that forgiving the person who hurt us will be freeing and healing. But maybe we just don't know how to get there.

Wanting to forgive is crucial—it's actually the first step toward forgiving.

Anger, of course, is an enormously powerful emotion. But like all our other emotions, it is not bad in itself. Even Jesus experienced and expressed anger—righteous anger, but *anger* nonetheless—for example, when he drove the moneychangers out of the Temple (see Mt 21:12). Anger needs to be channeled and, if appropriate, expressed in ways that are proportionate and adequate to the situation. Easier said than done, of course.

Sometimes, a certain amount of anger can and should be directed at the one who hurt us. It might seem counterintuitive, but this is not of itself contrary to forgiveness. Anger in the form of indignation is a reasonable response to any form of injustice—particularly when we have been on the receiving end of it. To *want* justice or recompense, to *want* a perpetrator to recognize his offense and ask forgiveness, to *want* just retribution—all of this is a normal response to hurt. Justice also benefits the perpetrator, and a good indicator that our anger is properly channeled is the extent to which it is motivated by a desire for this individual to rectify himself or herself.

But here's the catch: In order to heal, we eventually need to get to a place where we do not *need* that retribution, or that apology, or any recompense in order to recover and move on. Forgiving the perpetrator has the marvelous effect of freeing us from that need.

When I feel unable to forgive, or when I actually refuse to forgive, what's happening? Normally it means I am holding on to anger and clinging to a desire to hurt the offender in return. That unwillingness to forgive means subjecting myself to anger's control, allowing anger to dominate and bind me. As a consequence, the negative emotions—the resentment, grudges, ill will, or outright hatred, as the case may be—are all left to fester and intensify. The inability to exercise my interior freedom by choosing to forgive leaves the negative emotions in place, essentially untended, circulating in my psyche, multiplying and expanding their influence over me like a spiritual cancer.

In 1 Corinthians 13:5, St. Paul says that *agapē* love "does not brood over injury." Translated literally, that means love "does not take account of evil." Love strives to empty itself and leave no place for grudges, resentment, spite, or hatred. Does this seem beyond our human capacity at times? It should, because it often is. The power to forgive is a gift of grace, and we need to ask God for it. "To err is human, to forgive is divine." Indeed. Forgiving is an extreme expression of *agapē* love: "Father, forgive them, they know not what they do" (Lk 23:34).

My aim in this chapter, as it turns out, is not to *talk about* forgiveness or how important it is. Here, rather, I want to rely not on the power of explanation but on the power of *witness*. I want to share two personal testimonials of forgiveness that illustrate far better than any kind of expository writing just what forgiveness is all about.

Amy's Story

A very raw kind of emotional wound gets opened when we sense that we've been used, that we've been a means to someone else's end. That was Amy's wound. We spoke about it in detail, but she didn't want the details duplicated here because she wanted to protect the good name of those who inflicted her wound, in addition to keeping her own anonymity. But to give you some idea, Amy, a committed Catholic, had entrusted her time, talent, and unique gifts to collaborate with other individuals in a Church ministry. She loved these people, developed friendships with them, and shared her best with them in projects that were at the service of other hurting members of the Church.

But a time came when it became clear to her that what had really been going on—behind the scenes, we might say—was that some of these people were actually taking advantage of her expertise and know-how, in some cases, to advance an agenda and, in other cases, to advance some other institution or ministry. Amy was crushed by the impression that they were not so much interested in her or in reciprocating friendship with her; their real interest lay in what Amy could do for them, what she could deliver.

Once again, it was the ugly face of a Church that uses its members, and when done says "thanks very much" and "adios." Amy fell victim to a mindset that does not look to the most committed members of the Church as individuals, as friends, as brothers and sisters—but as cogs in a system, as elements that are "useful" for a cause. And putting cause over and above the person and the gift of friendship, these individuals hurt Amy enormously.

Looking back on her experience, with wounds that are still raw, Amy shared with me some of her reflections on her struggle to forgive:

Forgiveness has nothing to do with what I am feeling. It is a decision I make because I do not want to carry around anger, bitterness, and resentment, and most of all because I choose to do God's will and forgive in spite of what I feel.

Of course, this does not mean accepting continual unacceptable behavior if someone chooses not to change or try. I know I, for one, in my hurt within the church, did not want to see or believe what was right before my eyes. So, I set myself up to be hurt over and over again because I truly loved those who hurt me. But forgiveness does not mean allowing yourself to be abused emotionally or spiritually. It does mean letting go of the bitterness, praying for those who have hurt us.

It is not an easy task. There are days when I still question if I have truly forgiven. With a hurt so deep it probably does depend on the day and what circumstances I am dealing with since I cannot get away from the source. One thing I do know, I will keep choosing to forgive no matter how hard it is. I pray to be able to die to myself so that this hurt does not keep me from God in any way.

It is in times like this that I truly know what it means to be "brokenhearted" and how Jesus is close to us when we are. When we trust people with the very intimacy of our hearts, when we share that which is most dear to us and embedded in our hearts, and it is not treated with the respect and dignity it deserves, but is used instead for an agenda, it is very painful.

It is a true sharing in the suffering of Christ. I pray and continue to pray for the grace not to be resentful, bitter, or angry, but to make that choice to forgive, every day if I have to. It is hard when you are in deep pain, but it is a choice we need to continue to make because of our love for God, and because in the end that is what is really important, giving the mercy we have received.

Perhaps what struck me most during this was something I knew and heard a million times before, but through this it took on new meaning. Christ forgave from the cross! He did not forgive when he was feeling better, or when things settled down and he rose from the dead. He forgave from that very place of excruciating pain. He chose to forgive in the midst of his betrayal, of his physical and mental pain, his crucifixion! He chose to conquer sin with his love and forgiveness and mercy.

When we show mercy, it boomerangs right back to us: in a sense, we are being merciful to ourselves; we are unleashing ourselves from interior bondage. Which is to say that the exercise of mercy, in forgiving, transforms us powerfully within. Forgiveness, says the *Catechism of the Catholic Church*, transfigures the disciple by configuring us to the Master:

> It is there, in fact, "in the depths of the heart," that everything is bound and loosed. It is not in our power not to feel or to forget an offense; but the heart that offers itself to the Holy Spirit turns injury into compassion and purifies the memory in transforming the hurt into intercession.[30]

And as beautifully stated in the *Catechism*, "Forgiveness also bears witness that, in our world, love is stronger than sin." But for the individual—as Amy attests—to show mercy is to release a very real source of power that is spiritually healing, elevating, and trans-formative.

Megan's Story

Megan was sixteen, pregnant, and terrified. A cradle Catholic, Megan was attending an all-girls Catholic high school. Eventually—she doesn't quite remember how—she decided to have an abortion. Her parents knew nothing—only her boyfriend.

In the months following the abortion, Megan tried to pick up the rhythm of her teen life. But she discovered that everything had changed. And she struggled with what she described as an emptiness that just wouldn't go away, in spite of the initial assurances from her doctor that it was "just a question of hormones—it'll all go away." But it never did.

Attending school Masses, Megan would suddenly be overcome by anxiety and guilt—which she experienced as a sudden, almost suffocating rush of heat to her head and face. She was getting overwhelmed with the magnitude of what she had done, that it was a terrible sin.

It seemed there was no one she could talk to, and she didn't dare tell her parents. Then her cradle-Catholic upbringing shifted into gear: it occurred to her that maybe she could go to confession. She remembered: "that's what Catholics do" when they do bad things—they go to confession. "Maybe that will help me feel better," she thought.

∞

She described the school chaplain as "an older man." She doesn't remember his name. At the time, the school used the traditional confessional—the priest sitting in his own enclosed compartment, with two conjoined compartments on either side of his for the penitents. A large heavy curtain served as the entrance to the penitent's compartment. Once inside, the penitent would make his or her confession in a low tone of voice through a grill or screen that communicated with the priest's compartment.

Megan knelt down and began her confession. She confessed the abortion.

She believed that the priest on the other side of the screen represented God.

She believed God was merciful, and she was sure this priest would now show her just that.

But it was not to be. And what transpired next is beyond imagining.

Megan explained that, upon hearing her confess the sin of abortion, the priest got up, exited his side of the confessional, came around to her side, drew back the curtain, and confronted her angrily.

Megan—a vulnerable, and now terrified, sixteen-year-old—remained kneeling in stunned silence, looking up at the priest as he went off on a tirade.

"Do you have any idea what you have *done*? Do you have any idea *how terrible this is*?" the priest demanded to know.

Megan got up and attempted to walk away, but the priest grabbed her by one wrist, wheeled her around, grabbed the other wrist, and continued: "You are a *murderer*. Do you understand? You *murdered a baby*."

She repeated again that she was sorry.

"This isn't *about* being *sorry*," the priest snapped, emphasizing each word. "Don't you understand how serious this is? This is *not forgivable*. The only thing that you can do is get down on your knees *every single night for the rest of your life and beg God's forgiveness*. It's a sin that merits hell!"

And then he told her to leave: "I don't even want to look at you."

Those words—murderer, unforgivable, hell—sent sixteen-year-old Megan into a psychological and spiritual tailspin from which she would not emerge for the next fifteen years. The words haunted her. She had trusted that this priest would essentially reveal what God really thought of her. "So for me," Megan explained, "that's who God was. This priest had shown me who God was and what he felt for me."

She was convinced from that day forward that God was angry with her, that he was punishing her, that he wanted her to suffer.

She subsequently endured depression, anxiety, and panic attacks—which made it impossible to so much as step inside a Catholic church. "I can't go back there ever again ... I don't belong there," she remembered thinking to herself. And one thought above all was lodged in her mind: "I'm awful, I'm horrible, I'm going to hell."

She attempted to self-medicate with alcohol, drugs, and sexual promiscuity. She grew to hate the Catholic Church and everything it stood for. And she went on to have multiple abortions.

Eventually she sought therapy, and her life began to turn around somewhat. She married and had a baby girl. But her Catholic faith was still shattered. After her first baby, there followed a number of miscarriages. Megan recalls how, in one particularly dark moment, she addressed God about them: "Okay. How many more [miscarriages] before we're even?" As if God were evening up the score for her past abortions.

Over time, one of her therapists was eventually able to help her focus on the reality that she needed to come to terms with her shattered faith—and with her God problem. Her therapist recommended she speak to a young priest who had a reputation for being a gentle and compassionate man. She wanted Megan to get this priest's opinion about her situation. So at age thirty-one, Megan, for the first time in fifteen years (and now able to keep from panicking), went to church and approached the priest for confession. "Father," she finally asked, "can God forgive me?" To which this good priest replied: "Actually, God already forgave you a long time ago."

◌

After receiving absolution, Megan was still tormented by doubts. She went to many different priests, confessing her abortions over and over again. They all assured her of the same: that she was forgiven. She received their absolution time and again. But still the thought persisted: "What if *these priests* are wrong and *the other priest* [her high school chaplain] was right?" Eventually she met a priest who—with God's grace and much patience—was able to help Megan cut through the Gordian knot of doubts.

She began to meet with him regularly for spiritual guidance. Over time, in what seemed like baby steps, she began to let go of her many "issues" with the Catholic Church. She discovered that behind each "issue" there lay really only one fundamental issue that had imperiled her faith and poisoned her love for the Church: the anger she still bore toward that high school chaplain who had assured her she was going to hell.

Little by little, almost unbeknownst to Megan, God was gently healing her wounds and bringing her to a point where she could forgive the priest who had brought such devastation to her life. He did this by gently tugging at her own sense of compassion.

Megan explains how she was led to think that perhaps the priest's reaction was partly due to ignorance. She had had her first abortion only six years after *Roe v. Wade* had legalized abortion in the fifty states. Was Megan possibly the very first teenage girl this priest had ever encountered in the confessional confessing the sin of abortion? Or was she already one too many for this priest to handle? Megan felt that perhaps she had just been the object of all his frustration and disgust with society; maybe he was struggling to process the cultural revolution that had ushered in abortion on demand, and he had just unleashed it all on her in that one moment:

So, I found myself thinking that I was the "sacrificial lamb." And that idea—sacrificial lamb—led me to think how much we have in common with Jesus. I mean, when we're abused in this way, and we didn't deserve any of it, well, Jesus didn't deserve the abuse that he received. But it happened.

One afternoon, as she gazed at the crucifix, the words of Jesus—as he was being nailed to the cross—came to her: "Father, forgive them, for they know not what they do." And she thought: "I can apply those words to myself: 'Jesus, forgive me … I didn't know what I was doing when I had those abortions.'" And then another breakthrough came:

When I was finally able to take that from him … to receive his forgiveness … then I was able to give it to that priest: "You didn't know what you were doing, when you said those words to me. You didn't know how those words would affect me or what course my life would take because of those words." That was the key—to receive it from Jesus, and then to give it. And don't get me wrong. There was nothing easy about forgiving him. I had hated that priest for so long. But that's how I was able to do it.

By the same token, Megan emphasized that forgiving him did not mean validating or excusing what he had done:

Sometimes when we forgive someone, we use an expression like "It's okay." But that's not what we're talking about here. No, it's like: "What you did to me was not okay. But you know what? I forgive you, because I don't want you to have a hold on me any longer. I want peace in my life." And the only way we find that inner peace is by forgiving. Forgiveness is letting go. It's to rediscover hope. It's freedom.

As Megan and Amy have illustrated so well, forgiveness is not a feeling; it's a decision. But it is also something superhuman in a sense: forgiveness does not come naturally, and so often it is only with God's grace that we can do something which at times seems humanly impossible—especially when the perpetrator of the hurt is unrepentant. Even in the most painful instances, Jesus can give us the strength to forgive. And, of course, what can get the forgiveness flowing is to remember how often we ourselves have been the recipients of God's mercy.

Forgiveness, as Pope St. John Paul II has insightfully observed, seems so daunting precisely because it is paradoxical:

> Forgiveness is not a proposal that can be immediately understood or easily accepted; in many ways it is a paradoxical message. Forgiveness in fact always involves an *apparent* short-term loss for a *real* long-term gain.... Forgiveness may seem like weakness, but it demands great spiritual strength and moral courage, both in granting it and in accepting it. It may seem in some way to diminish us, but in fact it leads us to a fuller and richer humanity, more radiant with the splendor of the Creator.[31]

Forgiveness is paradoxical in the way so much of the Christian life is paradoxical: "Unless a grain of wheat falls into the earth and dies, it remains alone; but if it dies, it bears much fruit" (Jn 12:24). Forgiveness involves a self-renunciation that is at the same time profoundly self-affirming. In forgiving, we exercise an interior freedom that is life-giving and healing, and can go a long way to restore a wounded heart to wholeness. It can even mean at times the beginning of a new chapter in our lives.

CHAPTER 8

☞

The Healing of Thoughts and Memories

"The Lord replied: my precious child, I love you and would never leave you. During your times of trial and suffering, when you see only one set of footprints, it was then that I carried you."

—"Footprints in the Sand"

Our memories play an enormous role in shaping our self-understanding, as do our thoughts—our convictions, "certainties," conclusions—about our personal history. But memories are tricky; they can become blurred and misshapen. They can be painful—so much so that sometimes our mind actually suppresses them as a defense mechanism against the pain. Our thoughts about ourselves can accord with objective realities, or they can get subtly off course and lead us to embrace untruths about ourselves, about God, and about others.

No matter what happened to us, whether we've suffered a loss, or memories of past bad choices come to haunt us, or other persons have hurt us, an often crucial step in the healing process is to surrender our memories, and the very way we think about our personal history, to God.

God can bring healing to painful or deceptive memories. He can bring healing to thought processes that have gone awry. The experience of this healing is something like rising to a new level of personal awareness and self-understanding—like breaking through a solid gray cloud line into a blue sky and brilliant sunshine.

"God Makes Beautiful Out of It"

Best-selling author and survivor of sexual abuse Dawn Eden explains what can happen when we bring our memories to God:

> Memory is not to be feared; it is to be purified in the white heat of divine love. As divine love's light enters into the wounds left by past sorrow, we come to realize how the divine mercy carried us even during the times of our lives when we felt abandoned by God.[32]

This purification of memory can be essential to wholeness and healing, especially for those who have suffered emotional trauma. That healing requires at some point that we recover and reclaim a deeper truth about ourselves, about what was happening to us when we suffered—and about what God was doing in the midst of the hurt.

When I interviewed Megan—whose story of post-abortion trauma we read in chapter 7—she recounted how for a time, as she began to heal, she found herself "sneaking into church" during the middle of the afternoon when no one was around. Just sitting in church quietly was okay. It didn't cause her to panic. It was actually comforting. And her Catholic faith was kicking into gear again; she knew Jesus was there—sacramentally present in the tabernacle, behind the altar. She was alone with God.

Over time, memories began to surface during her visits, which became longer and more frequent. Some of her visits were intense and exhausting. She would cry. She would let herself get angry with God. She would demand to know why all these things had happened to her—how he could have allowed it all.

But as hard as those visits were at times, she always wanted to go back. "I would unravel my whole life before him," she explained. And she would look up occasionally at the large crucifix over the altar and gaze at the figure of Jesus nailed to the cross. And over time, as Megan puts it, "I got to know who he is ... and I just learned to accept his forgiveness. I was able to accept that he does love me, that I'm not going to hell." Little by little, the false image of the angry, condemning God was being displaced by a gentle, calming, loving Presence.

Megan shared, as well, how she had always struggled with wondering where God was the day this priest unloaded on her, and where God had been during her many years of struggle. She was led to consider how, in fact, she had become a very loving and affectionate mother of her own young children. She considered how she actually embodied and exuded a love and affection that she herself seldom knew as a child and adolescent. *Where had it come from?* How had she managed, in spite of everything she went through, to develop those traits? And then it hit her: It was God. He had been there, in mysterious ways, shaping her personality, molding her character, imbuing her with compassion, making her the person she has become today. "So, God makes beautiful out of it," she told me resolutely.

God enabled Megan to adjust *how she understood her own history* and bring it into better and truer focus. Again, as Dawn Eden explains, over time as we begin to heal, it is possible to "begin to see that even our most painful times contain beauty, inasmuch as they led us—however tangled our path—to our present life in the love of God."[33]

Healing of thoughts and memories was also crucial to my own recovery. In my own case, it was a process of bringing thoughts—convictions, really—about my past, and laying them before our

Lord, which finally brought healing to that aching hurt of "why did God let this happen to me?"

And it happened through spiritual direction. Deep down, I had been blaming God. After all, *I was the one*—I was convinced—who had given Jesus a blank check as an idealistic and committed Catholic young man back in 1986. Yet it seemed he had taken that check and made it payable to a group of individuals who would occasion the most intense suffering of my life.

One day, my spiritual director very wisely and gently took issue with my blank-check analogy. He was able to see that it was necessary to confront and correct certain convictions I had about my past. He challenged me to take a harder, more serene, and objective look at that past and ask myself: Had Jesus really written that check—*or had I?* Was it not rather my hasty, although well-intentioned, overzealous discernment process twenty-five years earlier that landed me where it did?[34]

After much honest and prayerful reflection aided by the distance of time, I was able to see that I had a large share of the responsibility here. I owned a good part of the cascading errors of judgment that impelled me to join such a troubled religious community. And as hard as it was to recognize that, it was also wonderfully liberating and filled me with a newfound sense of peace.

Most important, I was in a position to see that notwithstanding these missteps, Jesus was always the anchor. He was always the reason why I got up every morning during those years, and he was the one who accepted and made fruitful the oblation of my life, even in the misguided and hazardous circumstances in which I found myself.[35]

Yes, minutes, hours, days, *years* and my best energies had been caught up and sidetracked in the byzantine convolutions of what was in large part a religious sham. Yet Jesus had redeemed that time of my life. He had claimed it for his own designs and made those years fruitful. He had used me for the good of others. My life had had a point. *God had made beautiful out of it.*

Putting Two Very Contradictory Thoughts Together

Persons who have suffered personally devastating hurts in their experience of the Church—and for that matter, any person of faith who has suffered a personal tragedy—are confronted with one of life's most difficult challenges: how to reconcile belief in an all-powerful, all-loving God with the reality that, notwithstanding his omnipotence and benevolence, I or someone I love was left to experience something extremely painful.

It's the problem of pain, the mystery of suffering: God is love, and he loves me with an infinite love, and yet he has allowed me to suffer. Consequently, it's a battle of thoughts—thoughts which, depending on our specific hurts, struggles, and sufferings, can take a variety of forms.

Resolution of that problem usually involves a process of reconciling apparently contradictory claims and arriving at a higher synthesis of understanding and of faith.[36]

In the case of persons who have been hurt in the Church, those contradictory thoughts can present themselves in any number of forms involving God, his Church, and his ministers. Consider, for example, these apparently contradictory propositions:

Catholic priests are God's representatives ordained in the institutional Church to lead us to God.

And—

Hundreds of Catholic priests have sexually abused children in their care, and the institutional Church failed for decades in its response to these crimes.

Or:

The institutional Church has pledged itself to nurture me spiritually; to challenge, strengthen, and sanctify me for living the Christian life; to provide me a safe space in which I can be open and vulnerable, where I am welcome and wanted, and where I can experience genuine Christian love and friendship.

And—

The institutional Church has betrayed my trust and failed to protect me from the traumatic experience of ... X.

Zooming out even more broadly, we can see that these examples are simply instances of the broader problem of suffering:

An all-knowing, all-powerful, all-loving God loves me and never ceases to care for me.

And—

An all-knowing, all-powerful, all-loving God has permitted me to suffer.

Resolution of these conflicting thoughts is crucial to healing. Sadly, there are also destructive ways of dealing with that internal conflict which offer a false sense of resolution. We could respond, as many do, by simply walking away from the Church or by abandoning the faith altogether. That option leaves the apparent contradictions unresolved in reality, and leads ultimately to more havoc in our lives.

Proper resolution of the conflict is attainable only through a movement of thought and an exercise of supernatural faith that propel the believer into a higher level of understanding, awareness, and grasp of truth.

We're talking here about a gift of enlightenment: by God's grace, to be immersed in truths that, while remaining always mysterious and beyond our limited human reason, nonetheless provide us with a new certainty and clarity:

- Yes, members of the Church can fail us, and fail horrifically, but that does not detract from the holiness and goodness of the Church as a whole.

- Yes, some priests have committed atrocities against children who were left vulnerable by others in positions of leadership and authority in the Church, but that does not remove one iota from the truth of the Gospel of Jesus Christ, nor does it detract from the goodness, fidelity, and holiness of the vast majority of Catholic priests.

- And, yes, God is all loving and omnipotent, and yet, mysteriously, he has allowed hurtful things to happen to me or to persons I love, and from these events he has brought about a greater good.

For victims of clergy sexual abuse in particular, this process often involves pulling into an intelligible meaning two contradictory experiences: that of the priest perpetrator as someone who acted as a minister or instrument of God's grace, of inspiration, kindness, service, and—so it seemed—friendship, and that of the priest as abuser.

Resolution of that conflict in part will require the victim to process and embrace the truth that God, who is all knowing, all loving, and all powerful, is able to work around or in spite of profoundly troubled individuals.

Jean, whose story of abuse we shared in chapter two, felt, in spite of the abuse, that the Holy Spirit worked through the individuals and institutions of her local Church, even those individuals and institutions that succumbed to dysfunction, moral blindness, ineptitude, and ignorance—and failed to protect her. By God's grace, Jean was able to rise above the apparent contradiction, to a higher plain where she eventually received clarity, resolution, and peace.

Where Were You When I Was Hurting?

The healing of memory, the rectifying of thoughts—this is fundamental in the life of any Christian, essential for conversion, and crucial for healing wounds endured in the Church. Even the apostles—who relied so heavily on their memories of the experience of Jesus ("...what we have heard, what we have seen with our eyes, what we looked upon and touched with our hands" [1 Jn 1:1])—needed an infusion of corrective and healing insight into themselves and what had happened to them.

In their case, of course, it would take even more than mere insight.

The sadness and utter devastation of the events of Jesus' betrayal; his arrest, savage scourging, and crucifixion; the aching loss of the beloved Master that left nothing to live for; the painful memory of their own cowardly desertion of Jesus; the crushing sense of disappointment, dejection, and failure—all of this had to be dispelled by the brilliant light of the Resurrection, of Jesus himself, alive and risen from the dead: "Peace be with you....Why are you troubled? And why do questions arise in your hearts? Look at my hands and my feet, that it is I myself. Touch me and see, because a ghost does not have flesh and bones as you can see I have" (Lk 24:36-39).

Their memories and self-understanding had to be healed by the very palpable presence of Jesus—living, *present with them again*, alive, glorious and triumphant over death and evil, who would now give them his Spirit, send them on a great mission, and one day lead them home to heaven. Only in the dazzling light of the truth of Jesus' victory could they even begin to penetrate the mysterious ways of God: "Thus it is written that the Messiah would suffer and rise from the dead on the third day" (Lk 24:46).

When we hurt and struggle with thoughts and memories, God wants to give us a ray of that same penetrating light of the Resurrection. In that brilliant light, it is possible to understand that the

God who could have kept me from experiencing the hurt chose, instead, to accompany me in my pain and in this way draw me to himself.

In Michael O'Brien's magnificent novel-allegory *The Father's Tale*, the protagonist, Alex, has been detained under suspicion for spying and other alleged crimes—crimes he has not committed. After hours of interrogation and torture, Alex eventually loses consciousness. When he comes to, he finds himself left half dead on the ice-cold cement floor of a pitch-dark prison cell, naked, beaten, bloodied, his mind shattered. O'Brien depicts it all with a touch of Kafkaesque absurdity and surrealism that poignantly captures and conveys the inherent irrationality of human suffering. In the darkness of his solitary prison cell, at the most extreme moment of his agony, Alex notices a presence:

> The darkness was total, but it was broken by breathing that was not his own. He now realized that someone was lying close beside him. From time to time low groans came from the other's throat. Using the dregs of his strength, Alex moved an arm. It screamed in protest. He moved it still farther, and his fingers brushed against something. It was a hand. A hand covered with blood.... The arm of the other man moved. The man's hand reached for his.... With his other hand Alex touched the face of the prisoner. It too was covered with blood. The man's chin and cheeks were bearded, his nose large, his eyes deep-set.... His face was lacerated with many small cuts, and his lips were split, dry, parted.... The flesh of the forehead was riddled with holes....
>
> The prisoner reached up and took Alex's right hand in both of his. He drew Alex's hand downward across his face, over the collarbone, over the chest that was sliced in every direction, the flesh slippery with blood. He pulled

Alex's hand around the side of his chest and pressed the tips of his fingers to a large gash between two ribs. Alex flinched and tried to draw back, but the other's hands gently held him. "My son," said the prisoner, and drew the fingers deep into the wound beneath his heart. Then Alex saw a flash of light and fell into oblivion.[37]

Alex's encounter with Christ is iconic for what it can mean to discover—whether this realization hits me in the very instant of suffering, or only after much time has passed—that in the midst of my hurting, my God was there with me, the God who mysteriously permits me to experience evil, but who also just as certainly limits that evil, who does not allow me to be tested beyond my strength, the God who enters into my suffering to experience it with me, and for me.

When I interviewed Megan, I asked her what she would say to someone who is stuck on the why question: Why did God allow this to happen to me? Her answer welled up and overflowed from her own—now healed—self-understanding:

I would say to them: I know exactly what you feel like. But so does Jesus! Think about that! When he is on the cross, he even says it: "My God, my God why have you forsaken me?" You have to get to that place where you accept that you can't change the past; you can't change what happened to you. All you can do is go to that cross and say: "Jesus, heal me. I'm broken. I'm giving you all of this. I don't know what to feel about it or how to think about it. So, I'm just giving it to you."

Sometimes the insight God gives us about our own personal history, and our hurts, is not so much an illumination or understanding that helps us make sense of it all, but rather the serenity *to stop trying to make sense of it all*. It's the gift of surrendering it all to Jesus, bringing our wounds to his, allowing him to touch them, and discovering that Jesus is all we need.

A Yet More Glorious Day

God's healing and rectification of thoughts and memories is normally a very gradual process. And that process normally does involve struggle, especially when we grapple with the "why" of suffering.

It is certainly possible, with God's grace, to arrive at a heightened degree of self-understanding, of insight into our circumstances and our story in the light of God's truth. We can come to see the transcendence of the sufferings, setbacks, confusions, tumults, and upheavals we've endured as we survey that beautiful panorama of the lives of so many other people interwoven with ours, and all the good which God fashioned from what we endured.

Even when we have begun to heal, convinced and consoled by the truth that God is infinite love beyond all telling—all love, only love, all goodness, only goodness—and that he will bring good out of the hurt we have endured in our lives, that message, as Father Jonathan Morris has candidly noted, might still seem to fall short.

> But still, this is not enough. If we take all the human goods we have gained from suffering and add them to [the] spiritual goods, can we really say God has brought forth a "greater good" than the original loss?... So we don't have a solution—at least not a definitive one—to the problem of suffering unless someday suffering is no more. As long as we consider our fleeting life on earth our only chance for absolute fulfillment, we will logically always point an accusatory finger at the God of love and power.[38]

Complete healing, complete sense, complete meaning will be ours only in heaven. And that is God's promise to us. While sacred

Scripture assures us in big bold lettering, in both the Old and New Testaments, that our God is the God who brings good from evil, light from darkness, blessing from disaster, meaning from chaos, that he makes all things work together for the good of those who love him (see Rom 8:28)—this will be complete only in heaven:

> For man, this consummation will be the final realization of the unity of the human race, which God willed from creation and of which the pilgrim Church has been "in the nature of sacrament." Those who are united with Christ will form the community of the redeemed, "the holy city" of God, "the Bride, the wife of the Lamb." She will not be wounded any longer by sin, stains, self-love, that destroy or wound the earthly community.
>
> The beatific vision, in which God opens himself in an inexhaustible way to the elect, will be the ever flowing wellspring of happiness, peace, and mutual communion. (*Catechism*, 1045)

God's promise to all those who cling to him is that one day their hurts, and the Church's hurts, will all be vaporized in the all-encompassing fire of glory, when every tear will be wiped away (see Rv 21:4).

Before that "yet more glorious day" arrives, we will continue to grapple with the reality of suffering and the mysterious ways of our God. One of our greatest human possibilities, in fact, is to come to discover suffering as a pathway to union with God.

As we will explore in the next chapter, the great possibility held out to each one of us is to discover, as we share our hurts with our wounded Savior, an invitation to share his cross and his mission, to share in the mystery of redemption not only as passive recipients but as *active participants*, to unite our suffering to his redemptive suffering, to take up our cross and follow him.

℃

CHAPTER 9

Discerning a Call Within the Crisis

"The future is so much in the hands of God. I find it much more easy to accept today because yesterday is gone and tomorrow has not come and I have only today."

—St. Teresa of Calcutta

One of the best things we can do to help ourselves heal is to discover the new and blessed direction that God wants us to take, the new door he intends to open for us. That might be as simple as picking up some healthy new habit; it could mean praying more regularly; it might mean making time to visit an elderly, homebound neighbor or engage in some other corporal or spiritual work of mercy; or it could be as ambitious as a career change or launching a new organization. God often uses a time of crisis in our lives to invite us to just such new and positive ventures.

The word "crisis" comes from the Greek word meaning the turning point of a disease, a selection, a decision, or the outcome of a legal trial. So in a sense, "crisis" involves the notion that, from the onset of whatever the calamity might be, the results can ultimately break either way—for better or worse. The saying "every crisis is an opportunity" might seem Pollyannish. But spiritually speaking, at least, for the person endowed with Christian faith there's more to it than that. Much more. When we bring our hurts to Jesus, he can transform them into opportunities for excellence, for virtue, service, and mission that can usher immeasurable good into our life and the lives of others.

Discernment

If deep down we love the Church, and if we sincerely intend, notwithstanding the crisis, to remain faithful to Jesus, then we naturally want answers: Lord, where are you taking me from here? What comes next? What is your will for me now that the confusion and chaos have begun to subside?

To arrive at answers to those questions, to discover where he might be leading me beyond the crisis I've experienced, requires me to get on the same wavelength as God. It takes something called *discernment*, a word I have used often in this book.

The word "discern" is derived from a Latin verb meaning to distinguish or to separate out one thing from another. In the Catholic spiritual tradition, discernment is a process of doing just that in our own lives: distinguishing the influence and direction of the Holy Spirit from other influences in my life. It means my prayerful effort, aided often by a spiritual director, to discover God's will for me.

Discernment presumes, of course, a readiness to submit my will to God's, based on my trust that his will is what's best for me, and that he will in fact guide me to a knowledge of the best possible choices I can make in accordance with his will. It presupposes that there is more to "what's next" in my life than what *I* would simply prefer or determine.

Discernment, of course, is not a precise science. It requires patience for any number of reasons, but particularly because the "signs" I'm looking for do not normally appear according to my timetable, if they appear at all. And that's why it normally requires the help of an experienced spiritual director, because those signs are often difficult to detect and might not be at all what I am expecting.

As it often turns out, the fruit of good discernment, although it might seem counterintuitive, is not necessarily *certainty* that we are making the right move. Sometimes the Holy Spirit lets us experience a bit of ambiguity. But when we do eventually make the right move, the Holy Spirit will normally confirm this with the experience of inner peace. It's a peace which transcends mere human equanimity—the peace only God can give, a deep-seated sense of security and a humanly inexplicable sense of confirmation from above with regard to the step we are taking. It is an "Amen" from his Spirit to ours.

Now, not all hurts experienced along the journey of faith are so upending as to require discernment of this nature. But whatever the nature of the crisis, it is important that we always keep our minds and hearts open to perceive God at work in our lives precisely in and through that crisis.

God is very often present in these moments, inviting us to discover a new opportunity in the crisis, a new calling, a new invitation of his grace. Whatever might be his will, discernment is often necessary, and our readiness to engage in it is also a wonderful sign that we are well along the road of healing.

New Promptings of His Spirit and New Directions

In my case, it was not so much the discernment of a new calling as a process of elimination of potential options. "What was God doing?" I asked myself. "What was he calling me to do?" As my spiritual director and I opened ourselves to discern God's will for my life, we also sought the input, support, and guidance of trusted and prudent friends. Some aspects of where the Holy Spirit was about to lead me became readily clear almost immediately. What-ever would be the future of the Legionaries and the internal re-forms that they would have to take to rehabilitate their religious community—if that were even possible—I received no indication whatsoever that God was calling me to dedicate the years ahead to be a part of that re-foundation and reform project.

That being the case, I very much sensed the Lord leading me to initiate the process by which I would eventually be dispensed of my religious vows and be free to serve God in the remaining years of my life as a diocesan priest. This option was subsequently affirmed in prayer, in the judgment of my spiritual director, and by many other signs I took to indicate confirmation of God's will for me.

Peggy, in chapter 4, shared that in response to the hurt she was subjected to in the Church, she eventually sensed that God was calling her, as she put it, "to be the bigger Christian." By this, Peggy meant she was going to take the moral high ground. From within her experience of hurt she discerned a graced invitation to rise above what her baser instincts might have inclined her to say and do. She discovered an opportunity to grow in virtue by striv-ing to let go of the offense, by renouncing as often as necessary the inclination to harbor anger and enmity toward her pastor. She saw that God had dealt her the chance to grow in humility, and to trek up the moral high road by forgiving a man who was callous and embittered, and who had little idea of just how deeply he had offended her.

As well, Jean, Megan, and Amy also responded generously to a prompting of the Holy Spirit to share their stories, as they do in different venues, out of their conviction that God will use those stories to bring healing to others. And in so doing, they in turn have benefitted from experiencing further healing even as they contributed to the healing of others.

Sometimes the possibilities Jesus draws forth from our hurts flow beyond personal excellence and unfold as an invitation to *minister* to others. The Church is blessed with wonderful souls who have themselves struggled with past abuse or an addiction and then went through recovery and went on to establish new ministries and parish-based support groups. Some have published books or gone on speaking tours. Some volunteer. Some give their testimonials. Others have actually founded full-fledged organizations. Their personal experience of suffering and hurt led them to dedicate themselves to helping others heal. And here I think of my friend Miguel.

Miguel's Story

As a young man who lost his father when he was thirteen, Miguel was befriended by a Catholic priest. Sometime later, the priest, who lived in another city, invited Miguel to visit him. The first night he was there, the priest came into Miguel's bedroom, made unwanted sexual advances toward him and tried to grope his genitals. Miguel rejected his advances, pushed the priest away, and spent the rest of the night in a state of shock. Eventually, the memory of that night became buried, only to resurface in 2002 when news of the sexual abuse scandal in the Boston Archdiocese came to light. But it triggered other memories as well: his being sexually abused at age five by a mentally ill neighbor. Miguel began to suffer from nightmares, insomnia, and anxiety attacks.

Besides seeking professional help, he reached out to SNAP (Survivors Network of those Abused by Priests) and remained heavily involved in the organization for two years, partly because it was the only such network of its kind at that time. Many in the group were no longer practicing their faith, but Miguel was—his experience of abuse and the moral failure of this one priest had not destroyed his Catholic faith. But he was incensed by revelations of the Church's failed response to predator priests—and the steady trickle of revelations only contributed to his own worsening psychological state.

Miguel is now in his early sixties, lives outside of Houston, and is on disability due to PTSD. I first made contact with him by email, and that's how we corresponded over a period of a few months. When I finally suggested we speak on the phone or meet in person, he declined, explaining apologetically that he feared he would get too emotional, which would then trigger all sorts of things. Email correspondence was safest and allowed him to "keep control."

But eventually we did meet. He explained that ultimately he had to leave SNAP because of the hate and vitriol directed at him by members who couldn't understand how he could remain in the Church knowing the extent of the crimes committed and how they were covered up. But as Miguel explained to me, what he really wanted was to get over his rage and anger, and to help fix the Church—from the inside. He wanted to offer victims of abuse—whether perpetrated by clergy or not, whether sexual or some other type of abuse—a support system where expressions of faith were welcome, especially for abused Catholics who wanted to find a refuge in their own Church.

So he launched his own parish-based support group for victims of abuse. The endeavor branched out to other cities in Texas and is currently working on new chapters in Seattle and Chicago. Today, Miguel's Maria Goretti Network constitutes a prototype and shining example of just the kind of parish-based outreach to victims of abuse that could and should become a part of Catholic parish life across the country.*

---

* Miguel Prats is the founder of the Maria Goretti Network and lives in Katy, Texas. Visit his website at www.mgoretti.org.

His Wounds and Ours:
The Invitation to Redemptive Suffering

Sometimes the answer to "What is God doing in my life?" or "What's next in his plan for me?" does not involve major choices and decisions on our part. Sometimes it is simply to rest in the present moment, in the now of our life. This is particularly true when the direction we were hoping to receive from him does not present itself clearly. God also works this way at times, leaving us in something of a haze and inviting us simply to love as best we can, relying on his grace. In the end, we have only the present moment; in the end, all that is required of us is love. If I am striving to cooperate with the mysterious workings of his grace and to love others with the love that Jesus has poured into my heart (see Rom 5:5), I can be sure that I am pleasing him, that I am where I should be.

Such simple, day-to-day fidelity to what I think God wants of me in the wake of my personal crisis might not seem very satisfying. Perhaps I was expecting more clarity. Perhaps I still feel the need to make a change, the need for some big "move" in my life. And I feel as if God has just left me floating—in calm seas perhaps, but still uncertain ones.

It seems to me that moments like these are graced opportunities to discover, or rediscover, a much deeper calling, a much deeper mission that Our Lord extends to *every one of his followers*. And having experienced and survived a crisis in our lives, perhaps we are in a better position than ever, precisely because we have been so vulnerable and open to God's action, not *to do* something, but *to share in* something.

I am speaking here of Jesus' invitation to take up his cross and follow him, to suffer with him in love, to make my hurting redemptive by uniting my sufferings to his and sharing in his chalice of suffering. To embrace that invitation is, in fact, the core of what it means to be a "bigger Christian," to love better, to love more genuinely, to follow Jesus more faithfully.

In his homily during the canonization Mass for St. John XXIII and St. John Paul II, Pope Francis began with a reflection taken from that Sunday's Gospel, when Jesus appears to Thomas, the doubting apostle. The pope focused on that startling, confounding, and enduring feature of the resurrection appearances—Jesus reveals himself *with open wounds*:

> The wounds of Jesus are *a scandal, a stumbling block for faith*, yet they are also *the test of faith*. That is why on the body of the Risen Christ the wounds never pass away: they remain, for those wounds are the enduring sign of God's love for us. They are *essential for believing in God*. Not for believing that God exists, but for believing that *God is love, mercy and faithfulness*.

> St. Peter, quoting Isaiah, writes to Christians: "by his wounds you have been healed" (1 Pt 2:24, cf. Is 53:5).

The wounds on the glorious body of the risen Savior correspond somehow to the wounds of the Mystical Body. The wounds of Jesus are a scandal. The wounds that remain in his Mystical Body, the Church, are a scandal—including the hurts we personally have endured in the Church.

Much as when Jesus tells his disciples, "The poor you will always have with you" (Mt 26:11), he could likewise have informed them as well that "there will always be strife and divisions among you; you will hurt each other; you will fail miserably in your feeble attempts to 'love one another as I have loved you'; some of your members will commit unspeakable atrocities." There is a tragic and inescapable kind of necessity to it all—but nothing is left untouched by the mystery of Christ, by his wounds, passion, death, and resurrection. All is caught up in the great plan of Redemption, as Providence weaves grace and mercy into our personal histories.

In his encyclical on the Christian meaning of human suffering, *Salvifici Doloris*, Pope St. John Paul II wrote:

[W]hat we express by the word "suffering" seems to be particularly *essential to the nature of man*. It is as deep as man himself, precisely because it manifests in its own way that depth which is proper to man, and in its own way surpasses it. Suffering seems to belong to man's transcendence: it is one of those points in which man is in a certain sense "destined" to go beyond himself, and he is called to this in a mysterious way.[39]

His precious insight is that, with infinite wisdom, God has endowed human suffering—which mysteriously and inescapably remains part of the human condition—with a capacity to humanize us, to beautify and perfect us as human beings, and to become a pathway of union and intimacy with him.

By God's design, our sufferings—whatever they may be—can be endowed with a new nobility, purpose, and meaning when we unite them to Jesus. St. Paul is the great herald of the value of our sufferings united to Jesus:

Now I rejoice in my sufferings for your sake, and in my flesh I am filling up what is lacking in the afflictions of Christ on behalf of his body, which is the church, of which I am a minister in accordance with God's stewardship given to me to bring to completion for you the word of God, the mystery hidden from ages and from generations past. But now it has been manifested to his holy ones. (Colossians 1:24-26)

Reflecting on this passage, two millennia of spiritual writers have concurred: the way of perfection will lead the disciple of Christ to Calvary. If we are to be faithful to Jesus to the end, we must serenely and even joyfully embrace the truth that he will lead us into the experience of participation in his suffering. We cannot escape the "scandal" of the cross. The cross is a scandal to our limited power of human reasoning; it is a scandal to our human logic, to our visions and plans and dreams.

If we would truly be disciples and intimate friends of Jesus, then he will give us the opportunity to imitate and even share in his very self-emptying. This attribute of Jesus—*kenosis* in Greek (pronounced *kə 'nōsis*)—is set in high relief in that beautiful ancient Christian hymn that was incorporated into St. Paul's Letter to the Philippians: "Rather, he *emptied himself*, taking the form of a slave" (2:7).

Our sharing in Christ's *kenosis* is not only for our spiritual good, but also for the good of the Mystical Body. To share in his *kenosis* is to come to live that Gospel maxim which summarizes the whole mystery and adventure of following Jesus through Calvary to glory: "Unless a grain of wheat falls to the ground and dies, it remains just a grain of wheat; but if it dies, it produces much fruit" (Jn 12:24).

We should not be surprised when God invites us to drink deeply from the chalice of his Son's suffering, and to experience that loss of control, that turn-my-life-upside-down kind of *kenosis*! Admittedly, it takes loads of faith to recognize God's love at work in such moments, but they truly are privileged moments. We just need to be open.

Dawn Eden, reflecting on her experience of healing through meditating on the wounds of Jesus, puts it this way:

> When I unite my heart to the Sacred Heart of his Son, whose own wounds are now glorified, he heals me *through* my wounds. Through God's great love and mercy, my own sufferings become occasions of grace, salvation, and—most mysteriously—joy.[40]

The most fundamental and basic call within the crisis is the call to holiness, the invitation to follow Jesus more closely, to discover the paradoxical sweetness and joy of looking into the face of the Redeemer and discovering that he is right there with us in our hurt, that by uniting our own suffering to his redemptive suffering, ours can take on unfathomable meaning and incalculable value on a spiritual level which defies human comprehension.

The healing we can discover in the wounds of Christ is the healing of the *meaning and value* of suffering. This is something that he—and he alone—can give to our sufferings, when we surrender them to him.

Anyone who has been hurt in the Church can and should feel impelled, like Miguel, to help fix the Church and, like Peggy, to be a better Christian. In that interior impulse we can feel the workings of the Holy Spirit. There Our Lord is prompting us to help others heal, to build up a culture of *agapē* love where it is lacking, to examine—notwithstanding the wounds we bear—the talents and gifts God has given us. He wants us to do some soul-searching and ask ourselves: How can I be a better Christian? How can I be a more faithful disciple of Jesus? How can I help build up the Church?

On a deeper level as well, we can discover that more fundamental invitation of his grace to take up our cross and follow him, mysteriously and mystically uniting our sufferings to his. In this way, through each one of us, God can bring about an immense spiritual good for the Church—even if its palpable effects remain hidden from us.

Part III

Toward Healing a
Hurting Church

CHAPTER 10

༅

Continuing to Believe in
and Love the Church

*"If we are to accept the Church, we must take her as she is, in her
human day-to-day reality just as much as in her divine and
eternal ideality. If we are going to have the treasure, then we
must also have the 'earthen vessels' that contain it."*

—Henri de Lubac

The Jesuit Henri de Lubac was one of the greatest scholars of
our times, renowned for his gifted intellect and for the vol-
umes of potent and groundbreaking Catholic theology that are his
legacy. Yet he, too, shares with many of us the experience of having
been hurt in the Church.

In the years just after World War II, Catholic theology was experiencing a revival. Throughout the Church's history such reviv-
als have been fueled by intense debate, by often strongly worded
disagreements, and not infrequently by suspicions, accusations,
and polemics. De Lubac's era was no different. It came to pass that
certain of de Lubac's theological positions began to cause alarm
in the minds of some. His ideas became the object of suspicion.
The controversy finally rose to a boiling point in June 1950. It
was then that de Lubac, the brilliant and promising theologian,
was forbidden by his religious superiors to teach or publish. He

had to abandon his teaching position in Lyons, France, and was transferred to another Jesuit community in Paris.

De Lubac had been silenced.

In August 1950, Pope Pius XII published the encyclical *Humani Generis,* an examination and critique—according to its full title— of "some false opinions threatening to undermine the foundations of Catholic doctrine." De Lubac's most ardent critics claimed that it directly condemned one of his fundamental theological theses. Although the encyclical didn't mention any theologian by name, rumor had it that Pius XII was referring to de Lubac. Many within the Church's intelligentsia saw it as a very public rebuke of the Jesuit.

De Lubac, meanwhile, obeyed his religious superiors and bore with serenity and patience the wave of gossip and public humiliation that broke over him. In a letter to a friend that September, de Lubac wrote:

Although the shocks that assaulted me from without also troubled my soul to its depths, they are still powerless against the great and essential things that make up every moment of our lives. The Church is always there, in a motherly way, with her Sacraments and her prayer, with the Gospel that she hands down to us intact, with her Saints who surround us; in short, with Jesus Christ, present among us, whom she gives us, even more fully at the moments when she allows us to suffer.[41]

The silencing would last the better part of three years until his superiors suddenly lifted the ban and he was returned to Lyons with permission to teach. As de Lubac explains it:

During the whole affair … I was never questioned, I never had a single conversation about the root of the matter with any authority of the Church in Rome or the Society [of Jesus]. No one ever communicated to me any precise charge ... no one ever asked me for anything that would resemble a "retraction," explanation or particular submission.[42]

After his rehabilitation, many expected some form of retaliation on his part. But de Lubac was hardly a retaliatory soul, and certainly not against the Church. His next publication was his extraordinary *Méditation sur l'Église*—a series of meditations on this great mystery that is the Catholic Church. Begun years before his silencing as a series of meditations for priests, *Splendor of the Church* (the work's English-edition title) is written in ardent prose and laden with rich theology, yet tempered with the tenderness of a son writing about the mother he adores.

It was not the response that many expected from de Lubac after his silencing. One biographer observes:

> In his memoir, *At the Service of the Church*, he writes unsparingly about the conduct of his opponents and the weakness of many of his superiors. Even though in these lines he expresses his pain over so much injustice, mediocrity and lack of charity, his words are nevertheless free of bitterness. De Lubac's rejection of all later attempts to misuse his case as an occasion for criticism directed at "Rome" and ecclesiastical structures of authority is more harshly worded than his judgment on those who did him an injustice.[43]

Father de Lubac went on to play a pivotal role as a theological expert at the Second Vatican Council. There he would collaborate and form a warm friendship with a young Polish bishop, Karol Wojtyla. The latter, as Pope John Paul II, would make de Lubac a cardinal of the Church in 1983. With the help of this great theologian and faithful son of the Church, we will now attempt to shed some light on what can be a very vexing and painful set of questions for persons who have been hurt in the Church: How can I believe in the Church after what has happened to me? And even if I can believe with my head, can I still love the Church with my heart? I have especially in mind here those Catholic brothers and sisters of ours who have walked away from the Church and who would describe themselves as no longer practicing.

The very fact that the Church, in its current state, with her human imperfections, is a cause of dismay to us, that we are angry, disappointed, questioning, or distraught because of the Church—this is all a palpable sign that *we care*, that the reality of the Church *matters to us*, that it matters right down to our very core. We care and we ache for a Church that today more commonly displays its sinners than its saints.

Jesus, Yes. Church, No?

It's not uncommon these days, when discussing religion, to hear someone say something to the effect of "I believe in God; I just don't belong to any particular religion" or "I'm Christian, but I don't belong to any one particular denomination."[44] In the case of many Catholics who have walked away from the Church, a similar comment might be something like, "Sure, I still believe in Jesus; I just don't believe in the Church anymore."

Such persuasions are actually not new. Throughout history Catholic thinkers of many stripes have been tempted to fashion in their mind's eye a "Church" absent the external, hierarchical structure—and the feeble human elements which compose it. Theirs would be a "mystical" Church, one in which the visible trappings of authority and administration, which too often set the stage for conflict and hurt, would be stripped off. But to seek after such a

Church would be, in the words of de Lubac, "to refuse to follow the paradoxical logic of the Incarnation."[45]

What did he mean by that?

Our salvation has come about through the Incarnation of the Son of God into the real world of sinful human beings. The Church—as the Body of the Christ—must, as a result of Christ's incarnation, itself be incarnational: it is *and must be* present in the real world in and through its all too human, sinful, and fallen members.

"The Church," affirmed the Second Vatican Council, "embracing sinners in her bosom, is at the same time holy and always in need of being purified, and incessantly pursues the path of penance and renewal."[46] Today the Church experiences—as it has from the beginning—the tension between the holiness of her members and the need for purification, reform, and renewal.

Still, that might not mean much to a struggling disaffected Catholic. Trying to believe in the Church today can feel as if you are being sold a bill of goods. It just seems a risk too far: too many internal troubles, too much untoward history, too many scandals, too unchristian at times—too much to believe.

But if the reader will bear with me, let's take a closer look at what it means to profess belief in the Church.

"I Believe ... the Church"

The ninth of twelve articles of the Nicene Creed that Catholics profess at Mass every Sunday asserts the following: "I believe in one, holy, catholic, and apostolic Church." Here we need to take a close look at that expression "believe in." Unfortunately, the precision of the Latin formulation of the Creed and, in particular, its use of the expression "I believe in" (*credo in*) gets lost in the English translation. In English, we use the expression "I believe in" indifferently, applying it to everything from God, to one another, to UFOs.

Belief in the Church, to be sure, is not like believing in UFOs. It's actually not even like believing in the existence of Kalamazoo, Michigan: a place I've never visited myself, but that I take, based on the preponderance of evidence, to actually exist. Much less does belief in the Church mean a kind of belief that sets reason aside and turns a blind eye to history and learning. Believing in the Church is not merely a "leap of faith."

Actually, the Latin formulations of the Nicene Creed from the fifth to the twentieth century reserve the expression "I believe in" (*credo in*) exclusively for the first three articles: I believe *in* (*credo in*) one God the Father Almighty.... I believe *in* one Lord Jesus Christ.... I believe *in* the Holy Spirit.

As it turns out, when, in the Creed, it comes to affirming belief in the Church, the expression *credo in* is not used. A different phrasing in Latin—*credo Ecclesiam*—is used. If translated literally, it sounds awkward in English: "I believe the Church." (That's why we translate it as "I believe in the Church"). The meaning, however, is not "I have *faith in* the Church" but rather "I believe that the Church exists, and that it is one, holy, catholic, and apostolic."

It might seem as if we're cutting the baloney rather thin here, distinguishing between *faith* and *belief*. But this is actually an enormously important distinction for anyone who feels challenged by the prospect of believing in the Catholic Church.

By the phrase *credo in*, we signify a kind of amazing thing: an action which is at once human and divine, a genuinely free human act on our part, but at the same time an action which is dependent on God's grace. We're talking about the act of faith: an intensely personal, vital, life-shaping act by which I utterly entrust myself, my welfare, my past, present, and future—not to an institution or to any thing, but to God.[47] De Lubac captures the distinction beautifully:

You can believe in a lot of different things; but strictly speaking, you can have faith only in a person. Again, you can believe in personal beings too, in the sense of believing in their existence, and it is in this sense that we speak of belief in angels; but faith in the full sense of the word can have only God as its object, and this is the sort of faith that is meant by the expression "credo in."[48]

And here it would be helpful to recall as well that from the very beginnings of the Church,the profession of this threefold faith in God—Father, Son, and Holy Spirit—was linked to *conversion*. As Joseph Ratzinger/Pope Emeritus Benedict XVI has explained so well:

This means that faith is located in the act of conversion, in the shift of gravity from worship of the visible … to trust in the invisible. The phrase "I believe" could here be literally translated by "I hand myself over to," "I assent to."

In the sense of the Creed, and by origin, faith is not a recitation of doctrines, an acceptance of theories about things of which in themselves one knows nothing and therefore asserts something all the louder; it signifies a movement of the human existence … one could say that it signifies an "about-turn" by the whole person which from then on constantly structures one's existence.[49]

In a word, faith in God presupposes at least an initial degree of love of God, as well as our trusting self-surrender in his loving hands. It means committing ourselves to God, like an infant in his mother's arms. (The upshot of all of this as well is that to *believe things about* God is not yet to *have faith in* God. The latter requires God's help to bring about in us an act which is both human and supernatural.)

By the act of faith *in* God (*credo in*), and having rejected *evil and all that can keep us from God,* we turn to him in a superlative form of knowledge called *faith,* in which we lovingly affirm him and embrace all that he reveals about himself. To believe *in* God, as St. Thomas Aquinas beautifully puts it, is "to tend toward him in love."[50] This kind of "believing in" is hardly the schmaltzy, greeting-card-variety "I believe in you." Here, "to believe in" means *to have faith in,* allowing myself to be enveloped in the mystery of God and reaching out to him with unconditional trust. As de Lubac explains:

> In its fullest meaning, faith presents an ensemble of char-
> acteristics that distinguish it from simple belief. Of all
> modes of knowing, it is in itself, paradoxically, the firm-
> est and most assured, even though it always remains free
> and threatened.... It is an essentially personal act which,
> if rightly understood, involves the depths of one's being. It
> gives a definite orientation to one's entire being.[51]

Hence, *faith in* Father, Son, and Holy Spirit is followed in the Creed by statements of *belief* in what is necessarily entailed by that faith: belief in the Church, the dwelling place of the Trinity, the space where God reveals himself to humanity. Indeed, many early formulations of the Creed simply concluded with the article about the Church—as a conclusive receptacle in which the preceding articles found a fitting and logical culmination.

The New Testament, and the experience of the early Church, which is intimately coupled with it, indicates that Jesus intended to gather us into a Church that would be manifested over time not simply as a spiritual communion of believers but also with a hierarchical and institutional dimension. Consequently, the Creed that was handed on to us from the apostles suggests that *belief* in the reality of the Catholic Church is inseparable from, and actually flows from, *faith in* the God who reveals himself through his Son,

Jesus Christ. Catholic belief about the Church is beautifully captured in Eucharistic Preface VIII for Sundays in Ordinary Time as found in the Roman Missal:

> It is truly right and just, our duty and our salvation,
> always and everywhere to give you thanks,
> Lord, holy Father, almighty and eternal God.
> For, when your children were scattered afar by sin,
> through the Blood of your Son and the power of the Spirit,
> you gathered them again to yourself,
> that a people, formed as one by the unity of the Trinity,
> made the body of Christ and the temple of the Holy Spirit, might,
> to the praise of your manifold wisdom,
> *be manifest as the Church.*

So, if we are going to be faithful to that first nucleus of beliefs that the early Christians held to be necessary for baptism—*necessary if someone wanted to become a Christian*—then, yes, faith in Jesus has a lot to do with believing certain things about the Church he established.

An Appeal to Disaffected Catholics

What does all this mean for a Catholic who struggles to believe in the Church?

If the very prospect of professing belief in the Church makes you feel as if you would be selling yourself out, or engaging in a kind of blind act of fideism, is it because you conceive of that act of belief as a leap into an abyss—with no safety net, no support, with nothing on which to base that belief?

What I have just tried to explain is the *basis* for that belief, why it's safe to believe in the Church, notwithstanding the long history of all her human failings and miseries: We believe in the Church because first we have made our *act of faith in* the one true God, Father, Son, and Holy Spirit. Because, by the act of faith, I have allowed him to enfold me in his Mystery, because I love and trust my God, because he holds me in his hands, because he is faithful to his promises—because of *all that*, when God asks me to embrace belief in the Church, I can do so because of the firm foundation of my *faith in* him, and because I trust him utterly.

I am not inviting the disaffected Catholic to take a blind leap, or to "just trust" the Church's leadership.

Hardly.

Nor, to be precise, am I inviting you to "believe in" the Church per se.

Rather, I am inviting you, aided by that *divine grace* which will *not be lacking* to one who desires it, to make once again a fundamental *act of faith in God*—the God who has revealed his intention to invite and gather all people into his Church. With that simple act, you entrust yourself to him. And relying on *his strength* (and not on your own ability merely to espouse opinions and viewpoints), you can thereby renew *your belief* in what he has revealed—including your belief in the Catholic Church.

God can give you a new outlook and renewed strength to accept, tolerate, and bear with the human side of the Church, the earthen vessels that hold the treasure (see 2 Cor 4:7). If you have been hurt in the Church, he can expand your generosity, forbearance, and compassion to understand that the one who has hurt you is also a fragile earthen vessel, also a hurting member of the Church.

You might consider renewing your Catholic faith, now or at some future moment, by praying in these or similar words:

My God,
you are infinite Mercy, you are Love itself.
I love you, and I believe in you,
Father, Son, and Holy Spirit.
And because I believe in you, I believe everything you have
revealed.
I believe what you have revealed about this great mystery
which is the Church.
You know how I struggle. Help my unbelief.
Help me to rediscover the beauty, and goodness, and holiness
within the Church,
which is sometimes obscured and hidden by the moral
failings of its members.
Help me to love the Church not in spite of
but precisely because of her many human weaknesses and
failures.
Allow me to be your instrument
to help heal your Church.
Amen.

If you are not ready to make that act of faith just yet, my further appeal to you is this. Even if you have been hurt, possibly grievously hurt, in the Church, try to take baby steps, to open your mind and heart once again, even if it is just a crack, to the possibility of a renewed faith in God and belief in the Church.

For some of you, both mind and heart are currently closed—closed to giving any further thought to the topic, and empty of any affection whatsoever for the Church. Others might still have a kind of nostalgic fondness for the Church, and even a spiritual sort of attraction, yet still have intellectual problems with the Church. For still others, it's exactly the opposite: you remain open-minded, but you no longer have any heartfelt desire, no interest in or fondness for the Church. For one reason or another, you might still believe things *about* God, or even about the Church, but the latter is now disconnected from what you consider to be faith in God, if that itself has not been snuffed out by the harsh winds of life.

Whatever your situation, I make this appeal for one fundamental reason: We need you back in order to help heal a hurting Church.

Of course, in reality you are not "away." You are not "out there" somewhere. You are still members of the Church. You were baptized in the Catholic Church. It's just that for whatever reason you stopped practicing. We are still in this together, and together we need to heal, and help each other heal.

And the faith you have seemingly lost can be rekindled.

It's really a matter of wanting to get back to that place where your heart and mind are both open—and where you are willing to work through the issues that confounded your faith, or the hurts that repelled you.

There are different ways to go about making a return. Here are just a few suggestions:

- Have a heart-to-heart conversation with a committed and practicing Catholic friend, if you have one.

- Go online to find any number of helpful resources on the internet.

- Make an appointment to talk to a Catholic priest.

- Find a Catholic church near you offering a program such as "Discovering Christ," designed by ChristLife ministries.

Just make a move. God will be right there to inspire you and guide your steps.

CR

I remember a conversation I had once with a friend who is a lawyer for a large Catholic diocese. His work has involved him heavily over the years in a large amount of the filth that can gather in obscure corners of the Church. He's had to deal with fraud, malfeasance, embezzlement, as well as his share of cases of sexual misconduct. Far more than most of us, and on a daily basis, he confronts the all too human and broken dimensions of the Church.

At the end of that particular conversation, in which he was reflecting on some of his recent experiences, I couldn't help but ask: "Bill, you are exposed to so many bad things that happen in the Church. If you don't mind my asking: How do you *not* grow cynical? How do you continue to believe in the Church?" His answer beautifully captured that intimate relationship between *faith in God* and the *beliefs* that follow from it. He paused and then smiled and said, "Well, Father ... the Church is the Bride of Christ ... and *I really believe that!*" And then he added: "And God has been very merciful to me."

When we say "the Church," we mean so much more than the hierarchical, institutional dimension of the Catholic Church, its leadership and organization. When we speak of the Church, we mean the Bride of Christ (see 2 Cor 11:2-3; Eph 5:25-27; Rv 21:9), so united to her divine spouse that she forms one body with him who is her head, the Mystical Body of Christ composed of all the baptized.[52] We mean ourselves, the earthen vessels who hold the treasures Christ has left to us in his Church. "Us" versus "them" attitudes—laity versus hierarchy—much less an outlook that pits the spiritual dimension against the institutional reality, will never help the Church to heal.

It's not an either-or proposition for us. Together, we are the Church, and together we are called to be instruments of the Holy Spirit to build up that Church, to embrace sinners in her bosom, to contribute lovingly and faithfully to her ongoing renewal, and to bring healing to her hurting members.

CHAPTER 11

✿

Protecting Children and Safeguarding Victims of Sexual Abuse

"We might begin to deal with this issue by getting angry. Because if we are not angry, it means we really do not understand."

—Msgr. Stephen Rossetti

This chapter was hard to write, and I expect it will be hard to read. But it's a necessary chapter. At the very center of our efforts to bring healing to a wounded Catholic Church is the need to respond energetically and passionately to the Church's crisis of sexual abuse, helping victims heal, and determining ourselves to keep the protection of minors a vital priority of our pastoral care—today and forever. In this, we all have a role to play. But I begin with some thoughts on the paramount role that must be played by America's Catholic bishops.

Fifteen Years After Dallas

The *Charter for the Protection of Children and Young People* (the Charter) was adopted by the United States Conference of Catholic Bishops (USCCB) in June 2002 at their annual meeting in Dallas. The Charter (sometimes referred to as the "Dallas Charter") is a normative set of procedures for bishops when acting on allegations of sexual abuse of minors by Catholic clergy. It requires that bishops cooperate with civil authorities in the investigation of allegations, and gives guidelines for the disciplining of offenders.

At the epicenter of the Charter is the "zero tolerance" policy: when it has been established after an appropriate investigation that a cleric has abused a minor, he is to be removed from ministry—*permanently*.[53] It also outlines measures for the creation of "safe environments" for children and young people, for outreach to victims of abuse, and for the establishment of a National Review Board as one element of external accountability on the bishops in their efforts to protect children.[54]

The Charter was a watershed moment in the Church's response to child sexual abuse. Fully fifteen years later, the bishops as a body have created structures and institutionalized best practices for the protection of children and persons vulnerable to abuse. Individually, however, there remains a spectrum of attitudes, approaches, and responses to the crisis on the part of bishops—from those who have exhibited extraordinary pastoral presence and attention to victims, to those who sadly manifest insensitivity, inertia, and ineptitude.

Yet, fifteen years into the crisis, we must still question how many bishops *really* grasp the suffering endured by victims of sexual abuse. We should all find it disturbing, for instance—as one expert in the field who has worked closely with bishops confided to me—that few bishops show interest in being trained in how to minister to victims.

Fortunately, there is a growing number of bishops who are responding well, who get it—ones who have spent hours freely and willingly meeting with victims (and *not* because a judge required them to do so), listening to their stories, crying with them, and praying with them. As one bishop pointed out to me rather emphatically, he has been as angry as anyone: angry at his predecessor who mishandled abuse cases and covered up for predator priests, angry at the way victims were mistreated in his archdiocese, angry at the perpetrators—angry at this whole sad chapter in the Church's story.

One of the most healing things that any bishop can do for victims is to apologize on behalf of the Church—and do so often. Though on occasion legal settlements in abuse cases have required bishops to apologize or admit guilt—emptying such "apologies" of credibility and meaning—more commonly bishops have done so motivated by genuine sorrow and compassion, and their apologies have been candid and sincere. Some prelates have been inclined to ask forgiveness for the bishops as a body, and for their collective failures to protect children. Others have apologized for their own failures or for those of a predecessor.

I think, for example, of the words of Cardinal William Keeler of Baltimore in 2002 as the crisis was just unfolding:

> [T]he simple, painful truth is that the Church did not go far enough to protect children from sexual abuse … we have let our fears of scandal override the need for the kind of openness that helps prevent abuse. In the past, we sometimes have responded to victims and their families as adversaries, not as suffering members of the Church.

The words of Archbishop Wilton Gregory at the opening session of the annual meeting of bishops in Dallas the same year that would lead to the creation of the Charter were also poignant:

> We [bishops] are the ones, whether through ignorance or lack of vigilance, or—God forbid—with knowledge, who allowed priest abusers to remain in ministry and reassigned them to communities where they continue to abuse. We are the ones who chose not to report the criminal actions of priests to the authorities, because the law did not require this. We are the ones who worried more

about the possibility of scandal than in bringing about the kind of openness that helps prevent abuse.[55]

Yet, as the bishops readily know, words that do not lead to action on this issue are meaningless. The very credibility of the Catholic Church in the United States, its message and its mission, have hung in the balance for over a decade now as the bishops have grappled with how to respond to the crisis.

Priests, for our part, have to be ready to embrace the requirements of the Charter if ever an allegation of sexual misconduct were to be made against us, even if we know it to be false. We need to be ready to cooperate with the process, to step back from ministry while the accusation is investigated, and to be ready to unite to the cross of Christ whatever sufferings may come.

Accountability

As Catholic commentator George Weigel has aptly affirmed, "The Church of the twenty-first century must own the responsibility to deal with episcopal failures. It must do so for the sake of its own integrity."[56] Some recent surveys suggest that possibly as many as two-thirds of American Catholics express a serious lack of confidence that American bishops are responding adequately to the crisis.[57] Their credibility has largely been undermined by the apparent lack of mechanisms to hold malfeasant bishops accountable. And this—accountability—is what survivors of priest sexual abuse, their advocates, and Catholics around the globe have been demanding of bishops for years. At present, some slow progress in that direction has been made, but questions remain.

The Charter was significantly silent on the question of the disciplining of bishops. Technically, within the Catholic Church, the disciplining of a bishop is not the competence of an episcopal conference; it is the competence of the Holy See. But the broad perception—among laity and clergy alike—was that the bishops were giving themselves a pass. And well over a decade after the crisis exploded in 2002, that perception, in many sectors of the Church, largely remains: an episcopal caste that protects its own and follows a code of public silence in the face of a brother bishop's failures.

Pope Francis first gave a signal that bishop accountability was on his agenda in the summer of 2014 when he told a group of victims of clergy sexual abuse, "All bishops must carry out their pastoral ministry with the utmost care in order to help foster the protection of minors, and they will be held accountable."[58] Then, after meeting with another group of victims in Philadelphia in September 2015 on the occasion of the World Meeting of Families, Francis told bishops gathered there, in no uncertain terms:

> The crimes and sins of sexual abuse of minors may no longer be kept secret; I commit myself to ensuring that the Church makes every effort to protect minors, and I promise that those responsible will be held to account.

Already in March of that year he had established the Pontifical Commission for the Protection of Minors, a body established, according to its published statutes, "to propose initiatives to the Roman Pontiff ... for the purposes of promoting local responsibility in the particular Churches for the protection of all minors and vulnerable adults."

One of this Commission's most important initiatives was aimed at establishing clear canonical procedures for holding malfeasant bishops accountable and, where determined appropriate, for removing them from office. However, by March 2016 their proposal—although given initial approval by Pope Francis in June 2015—was stymied at the Vatican.[59]

In an attempt to resolve the impasse, in June 2016 Pope Francis took another tack. He published an apostolic letter clarifying what had been up until then an open question. The *Code of Canon Law* stipulates that a bishop may be removed from office for a "grave cause." Until June, it was unclear whether episcopal malfeasance in the handling of abuse cases constituted the kind of grave cause indicated in the code. Pope Francis settled that question in the affirmative: the mishandling of abuse cases by bishops will hereafter be unambiguously understood as the kind of offense for which a bishop can be removed from his office or asked to tender his resignation.[60] In 2015, in fact, two American bishops saw no other alternative than to submit their premature resignations from office due to their mishandling of clergy sexual abuse cases in their respective dioceses.[61]

The practical implementation and enforcement of Pope Francis' tweak to the *Code of Canon Law* remain sketchy and entail multiple unanswered questions—for example, Who has standing to bring a charge of malfeasance against a bishop? How does an investigation get initiated? Therefore, the pope's initiative has been met with extreme skepticism, especially by victims groups.

Their skepticism is bolstered in part by historical precedent. Even though canon law had for centuries enshrined well-established canonical processes for dealing with clerics who sexually abused minors, in practice, prior to Dallas, bishops often simply eschewed the canons, believing that their first response to the perpetrator should be "pastoral" rather than "punitive." Given the unique relationship between a bishop and his priests, the response to sexual abuse allegations in the Catholic Church has almost always been priest-centered, not child-centered. Focusing first and foremost on the accused priest, bishops—whether deliberately or by gross negligence—treated victims as mere litigants.[62] Only time will tell if, when, and how Francis' new measures will actually lead to greater real accountability on the part of bishops.

One bishop whom I interviewed insisted that the bishops *do* hold each other accountable far more than Catholics in the pew or the mainstream media realize. That's because it's done privately. He seemed to suggest, however, that bishops engage and challenge each other frequently and at times forcefully. That's good to know. Yet, it seems that credible episcopal accountability must come to require not only back-channel and private remonstration of a brother bishop, but *public and vocal* fraternal correction when necessary.

Confronting the Reality of Clergy Sexual Abuse

While the role of bishops on these matters is paramount, in reality every baptized Catholic, *each and every one of us,* is already heavily implicated in the crisis of clergy sexual abuse, and must take part in the Church's response. To begin to understand how that can be so, we need only recall these words of the apostle Paul in reference to the Body of Christ and its members: "If one part suffers, all the parts suffer with it" (1 Cor 12:26). But many Catholics resist such a thought: "All the priests I know are fantastic," "I don't know anyone who ever had a problem with a priest," "I've heard about these things on the news, but it's never happened in our parish," "Those things may have gone on years ago, but you don't hear about it so much anymore—I think we're past it." On the opposite side of the spectrum, of course, are those Catholics who have been so utterly scandalized by the crisis they have simply walked away from the Church.

We really need to ask ourselves: What happens when the Mystical Body of Christ is inflicted by an evil so insidious and of such incomprehensible magnitude as is the evil of child sexual abuse? The answer is that the evil impacts all of us—mysteriously, yet not insignificantly. Pope St. John Paul II once offered this insight:

> [B]y virtue of human solidarity which is as mysterious and intangible as it is real and concrete, each individual's

sin in some way affects others. This is the other aspect of that solidarity which on the religious level is developed in the profound and magnificent mystery of the communion of saints, thanks to which it has been possible to say that "every soul that rises above itself, raises up the world." To this law of ascent there unfortunately corresponds the law of descent. *Consequently one can speak of a communion of sin*, whereby a soul that lowers itself through sin drags down with itself the Church and, in some way, the whole world. In other words, there is no sin, not even the most intimate and secret one, the most strictly individual one, that exclusively concerns the person committing it. With greater or lesser violence, with greater or lesser harm, every sin has repercussions on the entire ecclesial body and the whole human family.[63]

A "communion of sin"—that's a tough concept. Not that we all share the guilt of the abusers, but we are all, at some profound level of our being, touched and spiritually harmed by this great evil.[64]

The Church community, having been brought into excruciating awareness of the scope and depth of the abuse crisis, cannot now shrink from that awareness and retreat back into insensibility. But historically, as researchers have shown, this is precisely what has happened over centuries both within and outside of the Church: a cycle in which a brief period of increased public awareness of the plight of sexually abused children is followed by a lull in that awareness and resistance to reform.[65] The specter of child sexual abuse is anxiety-provoking; we tend psychologically to want to keep news of it at arm's length.

We cannot allow the Church's now heightened awareness of, and sensitivity to, our cultural crisis of child sexual abuse and exploitation to wane; it simply must not give way to mystifying paralysis and inability or unwillingness to respond energetically, as was characteristic of the Church's non-response in previous decades.

If there seems to be a struggle within the Church—as surely there is—to overcome a mindset that resists placing *the protection of children at the core of her mission*, this would seem to indicate a profound and fundamental flaw in our own self-understanding as a Church. Decade upon decade of moral paralysis in confronting clergy sexual abuse, opacity, defensiveness and denial with regard to our failures, and resistance to acknowledging instances of cover-up and acquiescence—this all attests to that flaw, or, better, profound *wound*, in the soul of the Church.

The way forward for the Church in the United States must lead us through the painful passage of fully confronting the extent of the devastation unleashed upon the Church by the scourge of clergy sexual abuse. The process that countries such as the United States, Canada, Ireland, Germany, and Australia have already been through—victims coming forward, and the full scope of the abuse coming to light—is decades behind in most other countries of the world where the Church is present.

When, one day, the full magnitude of sexual abuse in the Church comes to light, we will finally be in a position to understand that this has been a kind of spiritual genocide taking place within the Catholic Church.

There can be no healing, there can be no recovery of moral stature and credibility for the Church, until we open ourselves to allow the full impact of the horror to touch us, crush us if it must, bring us to our knees, and force us to cry with the victims and scream in collective outrage.

Some of us have made that passage, but many, far too many, have not. Why is this necessary? For a very simple reason: so that it may never happen again, at the very least not on this scale. Sexual abuse is a scourge upon the world; its complete eradication is all but impossible. Our only hope of eradicating it in the Church is a fully lucid, deliberate, and sustained confrontation with what has been our tragic reality.

Educating Ourselves

That necessary confrontation with reality begins with education. Most Catholics need to begin following the issue of sexual abuse in the Church and getting themselves better informed about the Church's response.

In the summer of 2013, the U.S. Conference of Catholic Bishops commissioned the Center for Applied Research in the Apostolate (CARA) to conduct a national survey of American Catholic adults aimed at assessing their opinions and attitudes toward the steps the Church has taken in the United States to deal with and prevent the sexual abuse of minors by members of the clergy.[66] Some of the findings raise important questions, not to mention concerns.

Only 25 percent of respondents—whether they knew this outright, were making an educated guess, or merely speculating—answered correctly that "fewer than 5 percent of priests" have had "credible accusations of sexual abuse of a minor against them." To the same question 48 percent of respondents responded that they "don't know."

Twenty-one percent of Catholics responded correctly that instances of clergy sexual abuse were more common before 1985 and have been less common since. Fully 43 percent maintain (incorrectly) that such instances have been more common since 1985 or about the same as before 1985. And again, more than a third of respondents (36 percent) responded that they "don't know."

Also disappointing is that only 16 percent of respondents report having heard about the steps being taken in their own diocese to prevent the abuse of children—a statistic that has not changed in nearly a decade. And worse, 56 percent of respondents claim they do not know if the policies are being enforced.

That level of ignorance is damning.

Are the media to blame? In part. Bad news draws readership; good news doesn't. Are we getting the good news out there? We're trying, but our efforts come up short more often than not. But the blame rests as well with Catholics who simply don't care, who have not paid attention to the crisis, or who want to keep it at arm's length. There is no room for indifference here. Catholics have to care, and care deeply. They have to educate themselves in the causes of the crisis, and on sexual abuse prevention.

To be sure, in the past decade and a half since the crisis erupted, the bishops have made some solid strides in their response. As Msgr. Stephen Rossetti, a psychologist and international authority on clergy sexual abuse has pointed out, for example, in 2014 the Catholic Church in the United States spent $43 million on child abuse prevention and education alone. That figure did not include legal fees or settlement payments. Speaking to abuse prevention professionals in Ireland, Rossetti continued:

> To date, over 5.2 million adults and children have gone through the safe environment program in the USA. Every adult, priest, lay employee, or volunteer who has contact with children must go through the training. Criminal background checks are also used before individuals are hired, and over three million of these have been done. Every three years an independent secular firm is commissioned by the bishops to conduct a face-to-face audit on every diocese in the country to ensure compliance with the Church's Charter for the Protection of Children and Young People.[67]

The Church's prevention efforts appear to be having some effect in the United States. Abuse has gone down significantly, and admittedly our child protection program has become a model for organizations throughout the world.

Never Enough

Nonetheless, our attitude toward success can be laden with pitfalls. And the first danger is that, given fifteen years of making strides, we begin to rest on our laurels. Bishops must never allow themselves to ask: "But when is enough, enough?" We can never do enough for victims of sexual abuse perpetrated by clergy and others in leadership positions in the Church.

As long as our brothers and sisters, victims of clergy sexual abuse, continue to tell us that not enough is being done for them, that their crisis continues, that the bishops still seem largely out of touch, that they are discouraged by priests and Church officials who seem to think that we are on the downside of the crisis—then *that* is the perception of reality that *I need to understand*. And we as a Church must continue to find more adequate ways to respond to their sense of hurt, abandonment, and alienation. But, once again, it's our bishops who *must* lead the way. As Rossetti went on to observe:

> The Church needs more from its leaders. It is not enough simply that a bishop or major superior implements appropriate policies and guidelines, and deals with cases well. This is something a competent bureaucrat can do. We need them to be shepherds. We want them to lead. It is they who need to be charged by this issue and personally dedicated to protecting children. They need to be leading this effort, not dragging behind. We want our leaders out in front, calling us to follow the Spirit's lead in protecting children. This is their role.[68]

But going forward it will often be the victims themselves—like Jean and Miguel—who will lead the way forward and teach the rest of us how we can best respond.

Protecting children must truly be at the heart of our mission as well as protecting, nurturing, ministering, and providing assistance to victims. Here, perhaps, we will never be able to do enough. It requires many things of us as a Church. But at the same time, at least one of those requirements, one of those exigencies of love, is also quite simple: to accompany victims as they continue their journey in the Church. Again, Msgr. Rossetti, gets it exactly right:

> To stand with the poor and the victims, to become their voice and their companions, we must first listen to their pain. We must, as Pope Francis said, "weep" with them. At times we must become very angry at what they have unjustly suffered. We understand the sentiments of Jesus, who fashioned a whip of cords and threw out those who were defiling the Temple.
>
> This process will result in a conversion of heart. We listen; we become angry; we feel the pain; and we weep. This changes hearts. Today in the church I see glimmers of this conversion. Here and there, there are flashes of souls who "get it," who seem truly moved, transformed, and inspired to action.
>
> I have confidence that a day will come when the Catholic Church will be a refuge for those who are abused. The Church will be a mother to them, binding their wounds. The Church will be a father to them, raising a voice on their behalf. The Church will become their brothers and sisters, welcoming them into its family. [69]

We can indeed become that Church because God sent his Son to be our savior. We can become that Church if we open up wide to the power flowing from the wounded heart of Christ, who tenderly loves and accompanies everyone who hurts in his Church.

CHAPTER 12

A Revolution of Tenderness

"Remember, Lord, your Church, spread throughout the world,
and bring her to the fullness of charity."

—Eucharistic Prayer II

In the first apostolic exhortation of his pontificate—*Evangelii Gaudium* ("The Joy of the Gospel")—Pope Francis introduced the world to what is unarguably a central objective of his pontificate:

> The Christian ideal will always be a summons to overcome suspicion, habitual mistrust, fear of losing our privacy, all the defensive attitudes which today's world imposes on us. Many try to escape from others and take refuge in the comfort of their privacy or in a small circle of close friends, renouncing the realism of the social aspect of the Gospel. For just as some people want a purely spiritual Christ, without flesh and without the cross, they also want their interpersonal relationships provided by sophisticated equipment, by screens and systems which can be turned on and off on command.

> Meanwhile, the Gospel tells us constantly to run the risk of a face-to-face encounter with others, with their physical presence which challenges us, with their pain and their

pleas, with their joy which infects us in our close and con-
tinuous interaction.

True faith in the incarnate Son of God is inseparable from
self-giving, from membership in the community, from
service, from reconciliation with others. The Son of God,
by becoming flesh, summoned us to the revolution of tenderness. (88)

This pope wants to provoke a "revolution of tenderness" in the
Catholic Church. In a radio interview a year and a half later, after
announcing the Jubilee Year of Mercy, Pope Francis reiterated the
theme: "The revolution of tenderness is that which, today, we must
cultivate as a fruit of this year of mercy: the tenderness of God
toward each one of us."[70]

Maybe some Catholics squirm at the word "tenderness" and
find it suspect: too touchy-feely, too ambivalent, too fungible in
meaning, too open to misinterpretation. Won't some just see it as
code language for politically correct "tolerance"? How could so
tenuous a term give rise to a revolution? And besides, couldn't
the Church actually use a little more firmness right now, given the
moral chaos we live in, and the severe deficits in adult catechesis?
Shouldn't we be emphasizing the Church's clear and unwavering
moral doctrines?

A "Visceral" Love

I believe what Pope Francis has in mind is best revealed in sacred
Scripture—it is there, in fact, where he turns to further elucidate
what this revolution is all about. In an opening paragraph of *Misericordiae Vultus*, his letter promulgating the Year of Mercy, Pope
Francis observed:

"Patient and merciful." These words often go together in the Old Testament to describe God's nature. His being merciful is concretely demonstrated in his many actions throughout the history of salvation where his goodness prevails over punishment and destruction. In a special way the Psalms bring to the fore the grandeur of his merciful action: "He forgives all your iniquity, he heals all your diseases, he redeems your life from the pit, he crowns you with steadfast love and mercy" (Ps 103:3-4).

Another psalm, in an even more explicit way, attests to the concrete signs of his mercy: "He executes justice for the oppressed; he gives food to the hungry. The Lord sets the prisoners free; the Lord opens the eyes of the blind. The Lord lifts up those who are bowed down; the Lord loves the righteous. The Lord watches over the sojourners, he upholds the widow and the fatherless; but the way of the wicked he brings to ruin" (Ps 146:7-9). Here are some other expressions of the psalmist: "He heals the broken-hearted, and binds up their wounds.... The Lord lifts up the downtrodden, he casts the wicked to the ground" (Ps 147:3, 6).

In short, the mercy of God is not an abstract idea, but a concrete reality with which he reveals his love as that of a father or a mother, moved to the very depths out of love for their child. It is hardly an exaggeration to say that this is a "visceral" love. It gushes forth from the depths naturally, full of tenderness and compassion, indulgence and mercy. (*MV*, 6)

Yes—a visceral love. When God loves, he loves, as it were, "from the gut," from his infinite depths. The New Testament in particular captures and expresses this divine trait precisely because it is the essence of the superhuman love, *agapē* love, that the divine Son of God came to reveal and came to make possible. I believe it is a renewal of this visceral love in the Church that Pope Francis has in mind when he speaks of a revolution of tenderness.

And "visceral" is precisely the right word to use in English to get at the root of divine tenderness revealed in Scripture, which is often translated in English as "pity" or "compassion." In Matthew, Jesus feels "compassion" for the crowd, because they have nothing to eat and he does not want to send them away hungry (see Mt 15:32); he heals the two blind men out of "compassion" (20:34), and in a parable, the master forgives his servant's enormous debt out of "compassion" (Mt 18:27).

In Mark, the father of a demonically possessed son begs Jesus: "Have compassion on us!" (Mk 9:22). In Luke, moved by "compassion," Jesus raises the son of the widow of Nain (see Lk 7:13), the good Samaritan is moved to help the man beaten by robbers out of "compassion" (10:33), and the father of the prodigal son goes running down the road to meet him moved by "compassion" (15:20).

In the New Testament, "compassion" often translates a Greek word—the noun *splangchna*, or some form of the verb *splangchnizomai*—which in its etymological origins referred to the internal organs (where the ancient mind believed feelings were located), literally the "viscera" or "bowels." St. Paul, for example, tells the Philippians that he longs for them with the "compassion" of Christ, literally with the "viscera" or "bowels" of Jesus.[71] What the notion provokes and tries to convey is the depth of movement in the person inflamed with genuine Christlike love. It's a love that grips him down in his very guts; he is consumed by intense emotions, by the deepest feelings *for* the other and *with* the other: com-passion.

A Necessary Examination of Conscience

The revolution of tenderness means Catholics doing what it takes to better embody and make present in the world the tenderness of divine love. It means a return in some vital, life-changing way to the tenderness of God, allowing ourselves to be thoroughly steeped in that radical, visceral *agapē* love which is a gift of the Holy Spirit. Indeed, it means being open to the emergence in our faith communities of new gifts and charisms of compassion.

What we need as a Church is a new commitment to open ourselves to one another, not with a politically correct "tolerance," but with a radical empathy, and with a principled compassion that remains as faithful to Church teaching as it is passionate about doing all the good it can for the other.

How can the Church in the United States overcome an internal culture of hurt wherever it manifests itself? How do we break through a status-quo level of anemic charity and progress toward lives of more genuine Christlike *agapē* love? What can we envision for our local church, for our parishes and places of ministry? To what shall we aspire?

We can begin by envisioning our local churches as sacred spaces built up by members who genuinely care, who refuse to see their brothers and sisters as mere means to an end, who truly want the genuine good for each other. We can envision a Church of less self-absorption, one of greater virtue, of greater self-surrender, a Church that strives more ardently, seriously, and deliberately, at the interpersonal level, to make present the love of Jesus.

We can begin as well by undertaking a sincere examination of conscience. Here, we would do well to begin with prayerful reflection on some of the directives and reproaches St. Paul meted out to his first Christian communities. To the Ephesians he wrote:

And he gave some as apostles, others as prophets, others as evangelists, others as pastors and teachers, to equip the holy ones for the work of ministry for building up the body of Christ, until we all attain to the unity of faith and knowledge of the Son of God, to mature manhood, to the extent of the full stature of Christ, so that we may no longer be infants, tossed by waves and swept along by every wind of teaching arising from human trickery, from their cunning in the interests of deceitful scheming.

Rather, living the truth in love, we should grow in every way into him who is the head, Christ, from whom the whole body, joined and held together by every supporting ligament, with the proper functioning of each part, brings about the body's growth and builds itself up in love. (Ephesians 4:11-16)

As exegete Peter Williamson notes in his commentary on this passage:

The emphasis rests on the final word of the sentence both in Greek and in English. The Church can be strengthened only if her members conduct their relationships and fulfill their ministries "in love."[72]

Indeed. And in every age, local churches, to the extent that they fail to conduct their relationships and engage in their ministries "in love," become debilitated, spiritually emaciated. In a word, we need to heed again the apostle's warning:

If I speak in human and angelic tongues but do not have love, I am a resounding gong or a clashing cymbal. And if I have the gift of prophecy and comprehend all mysteries and all knowledge; if I have all faith so as to move mountains but do not have love, I am nothing. If I give away everything I own, and if I hand my body over so that I may boast but do not have love, I gain nothing. (1 Corinthians 13:1-3)

In turn, we desperately need to embrace anew that call to order he once addressed to the Christian community at Colossae—a call to that order, harmony, and peace which are meant to be the fruit of *agapē* love:

> But now you must put them all away: anger, fury, malice, slander, and obscene language out of your mouths. Stop lying to one another, since you have taken off the old self with its practices and have put on the new self, which is being renewed, for knowledge, in the image of its creator. Here there is not Greek and Jew, circumcision and uncircumcision, barbarian, Scythian, slave, free; but Christ is all and in all.
>
> Put on then, as God's chosen ones, holy and beloved, heartfelt compassion, kindness, humility, gentleness, and patience, bearing with one another and forgiving one another, if one has a grievance against another; as the Lord has forgiven you, so must you also do. And over all these put on love, that is, the bond of perfection. (Colossians 3:8-14).

In a word, if I want to contribute to the revolution of tenderness in the Church, I must begin by examining my own conscience with brutal honesty: how do *I* need to change? We need to examine, to search, to question ourselves, and to look to Jesus:

> The Church's first truth is the love of Christ. The Church makes herself a servant of this love and mediates it to all people: a love that forgives and expresses itself in the gift of oneself. Consequently, wherever the Church is present, the mercy of the Father must be evident. In our parishes, communities, associations, and movements, in a word,

wherever there are Christians, everyone should find an oasis of mercy. (*Misericordiae Vultus*, 12)

As a fruit of the Year of Mercy, things must change in the inner culture of our parishes, communities, associations, and movements. Am I ready to work to make my parish an *oasis of mercy*? My chancery? My office of priest personnel? My youth group? My liturgy committee? My parish council? My finance office? My religious ed office? My school? My rectory? My home? Am I ready to work patiently but consistently to expunge the cynicism, grudges, turf wars, intrigues, backbiting, and jealousies that contribute to a culture of hurt?

Maybe I need to call a complete moratorium on blaming others; maybe I just need to stop making excuses for myself, for my nastiness and impatience. Maybe I need to undertake a spiritual "cleanse" of all my negativity, bickering, complaining, and gossiping.

No doubt there are myriad ways we can be inspired to manifest Christ's love in the Church and in the world. We can all draw up our own very personal list of resolutions. We can and should make our own firm purposes of amendment because quite simply we can do a much better job of *trying*, of doing our part, to collaborate with God's grace and make Christlike love a reality in the here and now of our corner of the Church.

Yet we can't help but be keenly aware of how severely limited we are when left to our own efforts. The revolution of tenderness is not a personal self-improvement project. It's not about turning over a new leaf. It's not even just about "trying harder" to be charitable. The renewal of the life of charity in our local faith communities requires conversion of heart. And conversion requires God's grace. We must return again and again, in meditation and supplication, to "the Church's first truth," to the love of Jesus: "In this is love: not that we have loved God, but that he loved us and sent his Son as expiation for our sins" (1 Jn 4:10).

The more we have been touched by the love of Jesus in our own lives, by his tenderness and compassion, by his forgiveness, patience, forbearance, and mercy, the more easily we can then be empowered by his grace to make his love present in the world and in the Church—even to a new and revolutionary degree.

Every story in the preceding chapters is a story of someone who experienced the love of Christ, and, fueled by that love, was able not only to find healing but also to discover new ways of collaborating with a supernatural influx of *agapē* love and give expression to it in the Church. Such is the fruit of the conversion we presently and drastically need in the Church today.

As I bring these reflections to a close, I want to focus on just a few areas in particular that are in more urgent need of our attention, our conversion, and our willingness to collaborate with God's grace. They strike me as ideal starting points for launching the "revolution."

Minimizing the Impact When Hurts Are Unavoidable

Some hurts experienced in our walk of faith are unavoidable—in spite of the best of intentions, and all the gentleness and good will we can muster. In fact, there are some hurts in life—and within the Church—that are just part of maturing and will ultimately contribute to healthy psychological and spiritual growth.

To take just one example: there always has been and always will be the experience of negatives—a negative evaluation, a dismissal, a termination, a demotion, a reassignment, a rejection.

These have been part of the Church's experience from day one. When the apostles had to find a replacement for Judas, two candidates were identified: Matthias and Joseph Barsabbas (see Acts 1:21-26). Matthias was chosen; Joseph was not. Was that painful for Joseph at some level? Did it sting to some degree? Joseph was human; there must have been at least some disappointment to absorb, some sense of uncertainty, of adjustment as one proverbial door closed and another opened before him.

In the life of the Church and our participation in it, we will have some unavoidably negative experiences: plans changed, initiatives discarded, permissions denied, promises reneged. Employees will be let go; priests will be reassigned; candidates to seminary or the permanent diaconate will be turned away; school principals and DREs will be replaced. And the list goes on.

The vitally important question for our Church today is: Can't we do a better job at handling those situations? How do we allow these experiences to unfold—to the extent that we can control them? How do those negatives come packaged? What is the tenor and texture of a dismissal, a denial, a firing, or a termination? How are they presented?

Granted, for Joseph and Matthias, it was a matter of drawing lots—their election wasn't something personal, so to speak. Nonetheless, I can't imagine the other apostles being dismissive or shallow in their treatment of Joseph; I can't imagine them directing misplaced humor at him, or simply notifying him of his rejection without accompanying it with kind and encouraging words, without praying together with him.

Controlling Our Tongues in a Digital World

The word "visceral" connotes as well a kind of grittiness, forthrightness, candor, and directness. Our charity can, and at times must, be characterized by all of these things. Compassion must be principled, with firmness at times. It is not contrary to the revolution of tenderness for Catholics to give public witness in upholding difficult moral teachings (as we saw in chapter 5). It is possible to both "speak the truth" and to do so "in love" (Eph 4:15). The revolution of tenderness is not at odds with clear teaching. Tenderness and truth go together in the bigger picture of God's plan.

That being said, while genuine charity can at times require firmness on principle, and directness in our speech, let's look at the other side of that coin. I will venture that many of our faith communities could be practically transformed overnight if en masse we were to focus specifically on something that is not so much a matter of Christian virtue as mere human decency and, frankly, human maturity: the control of our tongues.

Apparently this too has been a challenge from the very beginning of the Church. Surely we are familiar with the lament of St. James:

> For every kind of beast and bird, of reptile and sea creature, can be tamed and has been tamed by the human species, but no human being can tame the tongue. It is a restless evil, full of deadly poison. With it we bless the Lord and Father, and with it we curse human beings who are made in the likeness of God. From the same mouth come blessing and cursing. This need not be so, my brothers. (James 3:7-10)

I leave it to the reader to think when and where and in what circumstances he or she is most vulnerable to fail in charity here. My own beloved father, a convert to Catholicism, would often point out to my mom and me how on Sundays, leaving church after Mass and walking to the parking lot, he could overhear parishioners already complaining, criticizing, or griping about something or someone—before they even got to their cars!

It occurs to me, however, that a particular area requiring our urgent attention is in our use of electronic and social media. On this count, I have failed many times—and my failures still haunt me. If you've lived to regret sending a nasty email or irritable text message, or posting a snarky Facebook comment or tweet, you know what I mean.

Particularly in the Catholic media, most especially in the Catholic blogosphere, to our shame, the medium of choice is too often vitriol. As Catholic author and commentator Jesuit Father James Martin once astutely observed, reflecting on the invective, disdain, contempt, attacks, insinuations, and downright nastiness that is too often passed off as legitimate Catholic commentary, "We risk being so Catholic that we forget to be Christian." Indeed.

There always remains a danger, in public cultural and theological debates, of closing oneself up in the satisfaction of *being right*. We engage in our polemics, and we slay our dragons; we spin out our blog posts and leave our nasty remarks in the comment boxes. We delight in being right. Granted, that's a caricature, but there remains always the danger that, to the legitimate task of engaging the culture and the world of ideas, there would fail to correspond the joyful, personal manifestation—not so much in words, but in deeds—of the beauty of the truth. The danger is closing oneself up in the self-congratulatory, self-referential satisfaction of being right, and failing to engage the world in kindness, in joy, in dialogue. The legitimate task of *speaking the truth in love* (see Eph 4:15) must always be complemented by our being *doers of the word* (Jas 1:22).

Today, committed Catholics need more often than not to endeavor *first* to *show* the beauty of the faith, rather than turning immediately to dialectical argumentation for the rectitude of the doctrine. It's not that the latter is not necessary, but it is not sufficient.

Making the Parish a Welcoming, Loving, and Safe Community

We cannot persevere long in committed Christian living without the support of a community where genuine *agapē* love is practiced in earnest. Our parishes have to be just that.

They must no longer be those places where we go to Mass and see the same persons every Sunday for years on end, sitting in the same pew, and yet we don't know a thing about them, not even their names, because we've never exchanged more than a passing "hello" with them!

How do I invite someone into a church or back to the Church where few, if any, are going to welcome that person? How can we usher them into an environment where sooner or later they might well be hurt or feel alienated? If we don't all agree on doctrinal matters, if some of our brothers and sisters who are returning have disagreements with the Church—we can get to that. The first order of business is welcoming, loving, and accompanying.

No Catholic—married, single, or consecrated, no elderly person in our communities, no professed religious, priest, or bishop, for that matter—should ever look around themselves and get that sinking feeling in the pit of their stomach, wondering whether there is anyone, *anyone at all,* in the church who *really cares about them.* No one should ever feel, in their service to the Church, that they are simply an answer to someone else's problem, that their existence is merely convenient for others.

And in our parish communities, a constant core concern of ministry must be the protection of minors and outreach to anyone who has suffered abuse of any kind.

∾

The revolution of tenderness—if it is to become real—can never be relegated to a special committee or task force in the diocese. It can't be the next diocesan program. We won't bring it about with pamphlets or web pages. This has to be the work of each and every one of us, or it will amount to nothing. It has to become an attitude, an approach to the Church and to everyone in the Church. The revival of *agapē* love in a robust, visceral, and daring degree can happen only in each of us one at a time. It means, in the end, to take seriously—very seriously—the parting words of our Savior at the

Last Supper, the new commandment of the New Covenant: "Love one another as I love you" (Jn 15:12).

That—to love with the love of Jesus—as we've already had occasion to reflect upon, is not just a tall order; it's actually humanly impossible. He alone is the one who can lift us by his grace to attain some degree of such an incredible love.

Nonetheless, we have to do our part to collaborate with God's grace. God does not force his gifts on us. We have to show an interest. We have to care. We have to *want* Christlike charity. It takes grace, but it also takes our examination of conscience, repentance, creativity, empathy, concern for others, and even grit at times.

We have to try, consciously and deliberately, to better our game at Christlike charity, so that Grace can capitalize on our efforts. We have to try to love with the love of Jesus. And in the present state of our Church, what's clear to me—and starting with myself—is that we can all do a much better job of trying.

We can and simply *must* do a much better job of trying.

☙

In these pages I've offered the reader the reflections of a fellow traveler along the roads of discipleship, in what continues to be the great adventure of being Catholic. It's an adventure I wouldn't trade for anything. To be sure, it has afforded me, like so many readers, unforeseen and unimaginable hurts; but so much more importantly the Church has been the instrument of every grace and blessing that the living God has bestowed on me in life. In the Church I have known Christ and learned to take up my cross and follow him, and discover the joy of that journey.

And that's the way it should be. Church is where we go to be nurtured spiritually, to learn the great story of God's redemptive love, to discover Jesus, to be challenged in our daily living, to embrace the crosses he permits, to be strengthened for the journey, to receive forgiveness when we fail, to receive mercy and grace, and to be loved unconditionally with the love of Christ.

Church should never be a place of callousness, indifference, and hurt—but, realistically, at times it will be.

Yet, we can all do something to remedy that.

We can examine our consciences. We can listen to the Holy Spirit, who will inspire us with out-of-the-box ways of loving our neighbor. It might feel odd. It might get us way out of our comfort zones. Things could get a little messy. That's okay. That's what happens when—lead by the Spirit—we push the outer limits of our self-giving.

He can show us how to whip up our own little "revolution of tenderness" in our corner of the Church. He can make our charity *visceral*. He can lead us to commit extreme acts of *agapē* love.

And if you have been hurt in the Church, Jesus can take you on a journey through your wounds, a journey of healing that will make you an even better human being, a better Christian, and a better disciple. He can turn your hurt into compassion. He can turn your hurt into tenderness for others. And you can even wake up one day to discover that what were once wounds have become amazingly a source of joy, a treasure-trove of wisdom and self-understanding—and a pathway to intimacy with God.

ભ

> Although the fig tree shall not blossom,
> neither shall fruit be in the vines;
> the labour of the olive shall fail,
> and the fields shall yield no meat;
> the flock shall be cut off from the fold,
> and there shall be no herd in the stalls:
> Yet I will rejoice in the Lord, I will joy in the God of my salvation.
> The Lord God is my strength,
> and he will make my feet like hinds' feet,
> and he will make me to walk upon mine high places.

—Habakkuk 3:17-19, King James Version

CR

"The High Places," answered the Shepherd, "are the starting places for the journey down to the lowest place in the world. When you have hinds' feet and can go 'leaping on the mountains and skipping on the hills,' you will be able, as I am, to run down from the heights in the gladdest self-giving and then go up to the mountains again. You will be able to mount to the High Places swifter than eagles, for it is only up on the High Places of Love that anyone can receive the power to pour themselves down in an utter abandonment of self-giving."

—Hannah Hurnard, *Hinds' Feet on High Places*

SOME RECOMMENDED READING

ೞ

For dealing with life's challenges, understanding yourself, and finding healing:

Conrad Baars, M.D., *Feeling and Healing Your Emotions: A Christian Psychiatrist Shows You How to Grow to Wholeness*

Kathleen Beckman, *God's Healing Mercy: Finding Your Path to Forgiveness, Peace and Joy*

Art and Laraine Bennett, *The Temperament God Gave You: The Classic Key to Knowing Yourself, Getting Along with Others, and Growing Closer to the Lord*

_____, *The Emotions God Gave You: A Guide for Catholics to Healthy and Holy Living*

Dawn Eden, *My Peace I Give You: Healing Sexual Wounds with the Help of the Saints*

_____, *Remembering God's Mercy: Redeem the Past and Free Yourself from Painful Memories*

Matt Fradd, *Delivered: True Stories of Men and Women Who Turned from Porn to Purity*

John Hampsch, *The Healing Power of the Eucharist*

Mary Healy, *Healing: Bringing the Gift of God's Mercy to the World*

Miriam J. Heidland, *Loved As I Am: An Invitation to Conversion, Healing, and Freedom Through Jesus*

Gerald G. May, M.D., *Addiction and Grace: Love and Spirituality in the Healing of Addictions*

Briege McKenna, *Miracles Do Happen*

Jonathan Morris, *The Way of Serenity*

For unraveling the problem of suffering:

Jonathan Morris, *The Promise: God's Purpose and Plan for When Life Hurts*

Hannah Hurnard, *Hinds' Feet on High Places*

For getting closer to God:

Gabrielle Bossis, *He and I*
Bert Ghezzi, *Discover Christ: Developing a Personal Relationship with Jesus*
Thomas H. Green, *Experiencing God: The Three Stages of Prayer*
Matthew Kelly, *Rediscover Jesus: An Invitation*
Ralph Martin, *The Fulfillment of All Desire: A Guidebook to the Journey to God Based on the Wisdom of the Saints*
Pope Francis, *The Name of God Is Mercy*

For nurturing your Catholic faith and growing in discipleship:

Dennis J. Billy, *Tending the Mustard Seed: Living the Faith in Today's World*
Cardinal Timothy Dolan and John Allen Jr., *A People of Hope: The Challenges Facing the Catholic Church and the Faith That Can Save It*
Thomas Dubay, *Deep Conversion—Deep Prayer*
Scott Hahn, *Reasons to Believe*
Matthew Kelly, *Rediscover Catholicism: A Spiritual Guide to Living with Passion and Purpose*
Pope Francis, *The Joy of Discipleship*
Milton Walsh, *Into All Truth: What Catholics Believe and Why*

And especially (but not exclusively) for Catholic priests and bishops:

Stephen J. Rossetti, *Born of the Eucharist: A Spirituality for Priests*
_____, *Letters to My Brothers: Words of Hope and Challenge for Priests*
Sherry Weddell, *Forming Intentional Disciples: The Path to Knowing and Following Jesus*
George Weigel, *Evangelical Catholicism: Deep Reform in the 21st-Century Church*

ACKNOWLEDGMENTS

༄

I'll begin by thanking every person who ever shared his or her experience of hurt with me, especially those survivors of clergy sexual abuse who courageously shared their stories. I thank His Eminence Timothy Cardinal Dolan for his constant encouragement, support, and keen insights into many of the topics in this book. Particular thanks go to Msgr. Peter Vaccari, rector of St. Joseph's Seminary, and to our faculty for offering me a sabbatical in the fall of 2015 to continue working on the manuscript—thanks again for "covering" for me; I am confident that the daily witness, the joy, and the wisdom that you have transmitted to me are present in these pages.

Special thanks are due to Monica Applewhite and Msgr. Stephen Rossetti, both international leaders in the prevention of child sexual abuse whose insights and reactions to early-draft chapters have been invaluable. Special thanks as well to Laraine and Art Bennett for encouraging me to write, and for introducing me to my editor Cindy Cavnar, to whom I owe endless gratitude for her dedication, candor, and editing prowess. And my sincerest gratitude as well to Enrique Aguilar, Father Peter Cameron, O.P., Father William Cleary, Father Roger Landry, Father Richard Veras, and Ryan Williams for reading earlier drafts of the manuscript or portions thereof, and for availing me of their invaluable insights and suggested improvements on the text.

Special thanks as well to Dawn Eden, whose writing has been an inspiration to me and a vehicle for healing for so many of her readers. To singer-songwriter and inspirational speaker Kitty Cleveland, whose voice and music so often brought me peace in the darker moments of my crisis—what a blessing you have been to so many of us. To Dorinda Bordlee and her husband, Tony, to Guy and Nell and my "NOLA family," my unending gratitude for your love and friendship, for providing the space where this book could get started—and for making crawfish boils, beignets, "Who Dat?", and *Drago's* a part of my life. To my *"famiglia"* at St. Columba parish: you really have no idea what your love, presence, and support have meant to me through the years.

My love and gratitude go as well to my sister, Kathy, my brother, Mike, my niece and nephews, and to friends too many to be listed here—you know who you are—but especially to those who accompanied me in their own unique ways during some particularly dark moments of my journey: Mike Augros, Christian Brugger, Maureen Condic, Father Stephen Fichter, Father Kevin Flannery, S.J., Robby George, Father Richard Gill, Michelle Gress, Markus Grompe, Father Joe Henchey, Father John Higgins, Dan Kane, Father Joe Koterski, S.J., Father Jonathan Morris, Eddie Mulholland, Declan Murphy, Father Steve Norton, Chris Oleson, Nik Nikas, Msgr. Sean Ogle, Father Peter Ryan, S.J., Father Anthony Sorgie, Father Luke Sweeney, and George Weigel. The journey continues.

ENDNOTES

℘

1. Sally Mews, *Inviting Catholics Home: A Parish Program* (Liguori, MO: Liguori, 2002), 31.

2. The Legion of Christ publicly admitted in late 2009 that the "Psalter of My Days" (in Spanish, "*El Salterio de mis Dias*")—a spiritual tract presumably written by Maciel between the years 1956 and 1959 when he had been ousted as general director—was actually a slightly modified version of an original work by the little-known Spanish author Luis Lucía. The discovery of such blatant plagiarism raised serious questions about the authorship of hundreds of presumed "letters" of the founder, questions which to this day remain unanswered, although it was already known that Maciel often relied heavily on his personal secretaries to write much of his personal correspondence.

3. In 1956, Maciel was investigated by the Holy See for accusations of theft, drug abuse, and exercising excessive control over the Legionary seminarians. The process took nearly three years during most of which Maciel was required to leave Rome. He spent much of that time in Madrid. Accusations at the time did not include sexual abuse. The investigation was suspended in 1959 under specious circumstances, and Maciel was reinstated as superior general. As a centerpiece of the grand narrative of the Legionaries' story, this period—interpreted as one of intense struggle with the "enemies of the Legion" and eventual triumph—would be referred to as "the Great Blessing." Any action by the Holy See on the accusations of sexual abuse that had surfaced in the late 1990s became stalled. Some previous attempts to inform the Holy See of these accusations in the preceding two decades had received no response. It would appear that it was only against considerable internal resistance at the Vatican that then Cardinal Joseph Ratzinger was able to launch a more formal and definitive investigation of Maciel in 2004. After Ratzinger's election as Pope Benedict XVI, the investigation—which was conducted under the auspices of the Congregation for the Doctrine of the Faith—was then left to that congregation's new prefect, Cardinal William Levada.

4. Both the 1917 and the current (1983) Code of Canon Law stipulate that when a priest absolves an accomplice in a sin against the Sixth Commandment, the absolution is invalid, and the priest is automatically excommunicated. The current code foresees as the only exception to the penalty the case in which the priest would absolve an accomplice in danger of dying.

5. In the summer of 2006, Maciel—who, according to the superiors, was beginning to suffer from dementia—traveled to Italy, to the small town of Termini near Naples, where the Legionary community would vacation, and visited them, accompanied by his mistress in full view of the community.

197

From October 2006 until his death, Maciel lived in a gated community in Jacksonville, Florida, where several Legionaries were assigned to live in community with him and take care of his every need. His mistress and the daughter fathered by Maciel visited him there on several occasions. Any number of Legionaries present there had to know who these two women were and why they were there.

As reported by the Associated Press, in a 2011 deposition, Father Luis Garza (then vicar general of the congregation) conceded becoming suspicious about the two women while visiting Maciel in Jacksonville in 2006. Garza personally verified in conversation with both of them that they were in fact Maciel's daughter and her mother. He even went so far as to obtain the daughter's birth certificate. Garza denied immediately confronting Maciel about the daughter. He stated that he only told Corcuera and two other priests. The article quotes Garza as saying, "I didn't think at the time that the fact that fathering a child would change in any way the way we needed to behave vis-à-vis Father Maciel or the actions that we needed to [take].... Because we needed to comply with indications of the Holy See and also because there was an issue of privacy and respect for the mother and the daughter."

6. The role played by Cardinal Franc Rode, prefect of the Congregation for Institutes of Consecrated Life and Societies of Apostolic Life from 2004 to 2011, well exemplifies that bewildering mindset. By his own admission, as early as late 2004 he was shown videotapes of Maciel with his mistress and daughter. Rode says he referred the matter to the Vatican official tasked with investigating Maciel at the time. While Rode credited himself with convincing or compelling Maciel to step down as general director of the congregation in 2005, nonetheless he continued to laud Maciel publicly on any number of occasions between 2004 and 2009. See Jason Berry, "Legion of Christ's deception, unearthed in new documents, indicates wider cover-up," *National Catholic Reporter*, February 18, 2013.

7. Father Garza has denied that any major superiors at the time were involved in any sort of coverup or tried to hide this information from members of the congregation. He attests, rather, that from the time their first suspicions about Maciel were aroused until the summer of 2008, they were working to assess whether the accusations against Maciel were credible. As of the summer of 2008, when—according to Garza—they were finally convinced of the truthfulness of the allegations, they began ever so slowly to inform members of the congregation, beginning with the superiors. After Maciel's death, a few elderly Legionary priests came forward and admitted to Garza that they knew of some of the things of which he had been accused. One explained that he never made a move to denounce the founder because he had no way of proving the accusation, and because Maciel was held in such high esteem by so many people.

8. See "The Legionaries' Last Stand: An Exclusive Interview with Fr. Thomas Berg," *Chiesa*, July 13, 2009; "The Legion's Scandal of Stalled Reform," *First Things: On the Square*, June 22, 2012; "Legion Reformed?" *First Things: On the Square*, January 14, 2014.

9. The cardinals assigned to carry out the apostolic visitation of the Legion's communities in 2010 were never tasked with investigating how the whole Maciel affair could have ever transpired, whether he had accomplices, or whether there was a coverup. Nor has the Legionary leadership to date been willing to allow independent examiners to engage in such an investigation.

10. Perhaps the most notorious case is that of Father Gordon MacRae. His case has been chronicled by *Wall Street Journal* editorial board member Dorothy Rabinowitz. At present, Father MacRae continues to be incarcerated after more than twenty years. From prison, he authors the blog *These Stone Walls*.

11. *Lumen Gentium*, 11.

12. *Presbyterorum Ordinis*, 12.

13. "If we try to contemplate God without having turned the face of our inner self entirely in His direction, we will end up inevitably by contemplating ourselves, and we will perhaps plunge into the abyss of *warm darkness* which is our own sensible nature" (Merton, *Thoughts in Solitude*, 48).

14. Press conference, returning from XXVIII World Youth Day, July 28, 2013. Available at: http://w2.vatican.va/content/francesco/en/speeches/2013/july/documents/papa-francesco_20130728_gmg-conferenza-stampa.html .

15. That teaching is quite well summarized in the *Catechism* in these terms: "By masturbation is to be understood the deliberate stimulation of the genital organs in order to derive sexual pleasure. 'Both the Magisterium of the Church, in the course of a constant tradition, and the moral sense of the faithful have been in no doubt and have firmly maintained that masturbation is an intrinsically and gravely disordered action.' 'The deliberate use of the sexual faculty, for whatever reason, outside of marriage is essentially contrary to its purpose.' For here sexual pleasure is sought outside of 'the sexual relationship which is demanded by the moral order and in which the total meaning of mutual self-giving and human procreation in the context of true love is achieved.'

    "To form an equitable judgment about the subjects' moral responsibility and to guide pastoral action, one must take into account the affective immaturity, force of acquired habit, conditions of anxiety or other psychological or social factors that lessen, if not even reduce to a minimum, moral culpability" (2352).

    How deeply this runs counter to the common secular understanding of masturbation as a normal, wholesome, and, in principle, morally neutral behavior cannot be exaggerated. The vast majority of lay Catholics—and a large portion of clergy and religious—for myriad reasons have basically embraced that secular understanding and become accustomed to living with a moral persuasion which they more or less know not to be in harmony with the Church's moral tradition, just as they often do with regard to the Church's teaching on contraception and homosexuality.

Some observations from the moral perspective are in order here given the broad denigration, rejection or at least misrepresentation of this teaching. To be sure, the Church teaches that masturbatory behavior—the stimulation of one's own genitals for sexual pleasure and the release of sexual tension—is what the Church refers to as "grave matter," an objectively seriously disordered behavior. But to be considered a mortal sin, such behavior must be deliberate—that is, it must be a personal act, the result of a deliberate choice. It must be engaged in with a pondered understanding of its gravity ("full knowledge") and by a willful choice ("full consent"). Lacking either or both of these latter two elements (due, for example, to immaturity, or emotional duress, fatigue, semi-wakefulness, and so on), the episode of masturbation in question does not constitute mortal sin, and is likely not even venially sinful.

Today, deliberate recourse to masturbation, with sexual fantasizing enhanced by internet pornography, can constitute a dehumanizing and destructive psychological cocktail whose devastating impact on relationships and marriages we are only beginning to assess.

It is certainly possible, however—contrary to common secular mischaracterizations—for celibates and non-celibates alike to strive to habitually forgo deliberate masturbation without experiencing psychological duress, scrupulosity, "suppression" of urges, and so on. The Church has long fostered forms of healthy asceticism that sustain the pursuit of personal chastity by various means, everything from rigorous physical exercise, to healthy friendships, pastimes, and amusements, to a healthy mental hygiene that seeks interior freedom from our sex-saturated cultural media. Such a way of life is possible with God's grace—particularly for the celibate. It is certainly possible to live a flourishing human life while striving to embrace every element of the Catholic Church's teaching on human sexuality.

16. As to the difficulties inherent in attempting to ascertain the incidence of priestly sexual activity, whether gay or straight, Mark D. Jordan has some substantially valid insights: "Compartmentalization and isolation characterize the sexual lives of most [sexually active] Catholic clergyman of whatever orientation, but the compartmentalization is particularly strict when it comes to homosexual relations. [And] … no one knows more than a few of the compartments. The church is not one big closet. It is a honeycomb of closets that no one can survey in its entirety.… [Consequently] there is no suite of inner rooms sheltering all the gay clergy. There are no well-established rituals or sweeping histories or even enduring networks of support. There is no *inside*. The varieties of sexual lives in the clergy are too complicated and too compartmentalized." *The Silence of Sodom: Homosexuality in the Modern Catholicism* (Chicago: University of Chicago Press, 2000), 89, 91.

17. *Optatam Totius*, 14.

18. Henri de Lubac, *The Splendor of the Church* (New York: Sheed & Ward, 1956), 203.
19. See *Gaudium et Spes*, 24.
20. He also observed: "I prefer that homosexuals come to confession, that they stay close to the Lord, and that we pray all together. You can advise them to pray, show goodwill, show them the way, and accompany them along it." The clarification was published in Pope Francis' *The Name of God Is Mercy: A Conversation with Andrea Tornielli* (New York: Random House, 2016), 61-62.
21. And we could cite any number of other passages, especially from St. Paul. Two examples in particular touch on issues related to sexual behavior: "As for yourself, you must say what is consistent with sound doctrine, namely, that older men should be temperate, dignified, self-controlled, sound in faith, love, and endurance. Similarly, older women should be reverent in their behavior, not slanderers, not addicted to drink, teaching what is good, so that they may train younger women to love their husbands and children, to be self-controlled, chaste, good homemakers, under the control of their husbands, so that the word of God may not be discredited. Urge the younger men, similarly, to control themselves" (Ti 2:1-6); and: "Therefore, sin must not reign over your mortal bodies so that you obey their desires. And do not present the parts of your bodies to sin as weapons for wickedness, but present yourselves to God as raised from the dead to life and the parts of your bodies to God as weapons for righteousness" (Rom 6:12-13).
22. This has long been understood and formulated in the sphere of canon law and moral theology in the Latin expression *de internis neque Ecclesia iudicat*, meaning, "of the interior dispositions of a person, not even the Church may judge." But this principle has never been understood to preclude the moral assessment of objective behaviors, or even of another's intentions (understood that, with regard to the latter, our capacity is drastically limited).
23. Dr. Paul McHugh, former psychiatrist in chief at Johns Hopkins Hospital took to the pages of the *Wall Street Journal* a few years ago to explain why his institution ceased performing sex-reassignment surgery: "We at Johns Hopkins University—which in the 1960s was the first American medical center to venture into 'sex-reassignment surgery'—launched a study in the 1970s comparing the outcomes of transgendered people who had the surgery with the outcomes of those who did not. Most of the surgically treated patients described themselves as 'satisfied' by the results, but their subsequent psycho-social adjustments were no better than those who didn't have the surgery. And so at Hopkins we stopped doing sex-reassignment surgery, since producing a "satisfied" but still troubled patient seemed an inadequate reason for surgically amputating normal organs ("Transgender Surgery Isn't the Solution," *Wall Street Journal*, June 12, 2014). See also Lawrence S. Mayer, M.B, M.S., Ph.D., and Paul R. McHugh, M.D., "Sexuality and Gender: Findings from the Biological, Psychological, and Social Sciences, *The New Atlantis* 50 (Fall 2016), 4-143.

24. http://www.gallup.com/poll/183383/americans-greatly-overestimate-per-cent-gay-lesbian.aspx.

25. http://www.pewresearch.org/fact-tank/2014/10/16/young-u-s-catholics-overwhelmingly-accepting-of-homosexuality/

26. The official Vatican translation of Pope Francis' on-board answer to the question while returning from his apostolic mission to Armenia reads in part: "There are traditions in some countries, in some cultures that have a different mentality on this problem. I think that the Church must not only ask forgiveness from the gay person who is offended, but she must also ask for forgiveness from the poor too, from women who are exploited, from children who are exploited for labour. She must ask forgiveness for having blessed so many weapons. The Church must ask forgiveness for often not be-having well—when I say the Church, I mean Christians. The Church is holy, we are sinners. Christians must ask forgiveness for having not accompanied so many choices, and so many families.... I remember from my childhood, the culture in Buenos Aires, the closed Catholic culture. I come from there. You couldn't enter the house of a divorced family; I'm speaking of 80 years ago. The culture has changed, thanks be to God. Christians must apologise for many things, and not just this."

27. See especially Eve Tushnet, *Gay and Catholic: Accepting My Sexuality, Finding Community, Living My Faith* (Notre Dame, IN: Ave Maria Press, 2014).

28. It is beyond the scope of the present volume to explore those reasons here, but resources are not lacking for Catholics who sincerely want to under-stand the Church's teaching on human sexuality in greater depth. I would recommend, for example: Gregory Popcak, *Holy Sex! A Catholic Guide to Toe-Curling, Mind-Blowing, Infallible Loving* (Spring Valley, NY: Crossroad, 2008); and Christopher West, *Theology of the Body for Beginners: A Basic Introduction to Pope John Paul II's Sexual Revolution, Revised Edition* (West Chester, PA: Ascension Press, 2009).

29. Art and Laraine Bennett, *The Emotions God Gave You: A Guide for Catholics to Healthy and Holy Living* (Frederick, MD: The Word Among Us Press, 2011), 123-124. This is an excellent resource for personal growth, particu-larly for those who find themselves in need of emotional healing.

30. See *Catechism of the Catholic Church*, 2843-44.

31. Pope John Paul II, Message for the Celebration of the World Day of Peace, January 1, 2002.

32. Dawn Eden, *My Peace I Give You: Healing Sexual Wounds with the Help of the Saints* (Notre Dame, IN: Ave Maria Press, 2012), 75. See also her *Remembering God's Mercy: Redeem the Past and Free Yourself from Painful Memories* (Notre Dame, IN: Ave Maria Press, 2016). Both books constitute an enormous resource for any victim of sexual abuse who seeks healing of past wounds and especially of memories.

33. *My Peace I Give You*, 44.

34. After *only two weeks* in a postulancy program in Spain in the summer of 1986, I believed I had discerned a "call" to enter the Legionaries. I dropped out of Marquette University after having completed my junior year, abandoned my native Milwaukee, and was admitted to a two-year Legionary novitiate in Cheshire, Connecticut. There the superiors instilled in us the conviction that one "has the vocation" to the Legion until told otherwise by the superiors. Like so many Legionaries who remained for years in the congregation, our "discernment" of a calling to the Legionaries was severely compromised, while our personal generosity was leveraged and manipulated in a web of deceptions. In reality, there never was, at any point in my own experience of the Legion, the solid and sure ground on which to freely discern some kind of call to the congregation. I even recall that at one point, at the very beginning of postulancy, I actually confronted the director—a priest who himself left the Legionaries in the mid-1990s—and shared my concern that some of the activities felt cult-like; I was worried someone was trying to brainwash us. Other men, both those who have abandoned the congregation and others who have remained, will disagree with me here and speak of their discernment of a "Legionary vocation" as a very genuine experience of the Holy Spirit's guidance in their lives. Still others who were ordained priests as Legionaries—and who subsequently left, and requested laicization—reflect back on an experience of having supposedly discerned a "calling" to the Legion, but not to the priesthood.

35. The Legionaries have not as yet been willing to embrace and actively pursue a full accounting of their own history. For their own healing as a congregation, and to further the healing of those who have been hurt in their relationship with the Legionaries and Regnum Christi, a full, transparent encounter and reckoning with their own history remains a paramount necessity. This would best be accomplished if the Legionaries were to constitute a fully independent panel of experts and grant them full access to the congregation's archives. The Church cannot fully recover from the unprecedented scandal of the Maciel affair without such a full accounting of just how this chapter in the Church's history could have ever unfolded.

36. Stephen Rossetti aptly describes how such resolution can come about, taking as an example a lay Catholic's struggle to assimilate the reality of clergy sexual abuse in the Church: "In order to resolve this crisis, the two conflicting realities must be juxtaposed and then synthesized into a higher resolution. The two apparently conflicting truths are: (1) 'Some priests have sexually abused children and the institutional Church has not always responded well' and (2) 'Priests and the institutional Catholic Church are symbols of the Divine.' Can these two statements both be true?... In the latter stages of faith, the believer accepts that sometimes deeply flawed human beings and religious institutions can be channels of divine grace. The person of the priest and the religious institution are, at once, sinner and vessel of grace. In later stages, allegations of clerical sexual abuse or inappropriate

Church response might cause the believer to be outraged and/or saddened, but they do not cause a crisis of faith." Stephen J. Rossetti, *A Tragic Grace* (Collegeville, MN: Liturgical Press, 1996), 97-98.

37. Michael O'Brien, *The Father's Tale* (San Francisco: Ignatius Press, 2011), 929.

38. Jonathan Morris, *The Promise: God's Purpose and Plan for When Life Hurts* (New York: HarperCollins, 2008), 75-77.

39. *Salvifici Doloris*, 2.

40. *My Peace I Give You*, 117-118.

41. Rudolf Voderholzer, *Meet Henri de Lubac* (San Francisco: Ignatius, 2008), 73.

42. Henri de Lubac, *At the Service of the Church* (San Francisco: Ignatius, 1993), 78.

43. *Meet Henri de Lubac*, 63.

44. Catholics, as a segment of the U.S. population, shrank by 3.1 percent from 2007 to 2014, and are now outnumbered as a portion of the American population by the "nones," the religiously unaffiliated, according to the Pew Research Center's 2014 "Religious Landscape Study" published in 2015. Paradoxically, the same study showed that in 2014, fully 49 percent of religiously unaffiliated Americans described their belief in God as "absolutely certain" or "fairly certain."

45. Henri de Lubac, *The Splendor of the Church* (San Francisco: Ignatius Press, 1999), 88.

46. *Lumen Gentium*, 8.

47. St. Thomas Aquinas, synthesizing centuries of Catholic teaching, taught that the act of faith "is an act of the intellect assenting to the divine truth by command of the will moved by God through grace" (*Summa Thelogica,* II-II, q. 2, a. 9). With the tradition that preceded him, he taught that the act of faith includes three movements, as it were: believing that a God exists (*credere deum*), believing this by virtue of God himself and what he reveals (*credere deo*), and, finally, entrusting myself to God as I believe in him (*credere in deum*). See *S.T.*, II-II, q. 2, a. 2.

As theologian Hans Urs von Balthasar explains: "Thus we find, in the case of the Fathers, a distinguishing (constantly repeated all the way into the Middle Ages) of three levels within the act of faith, with only the third representing faith in its total fullness: *credere Deum* (belief that God exists), *credere Deo* (belief in what God says), *credere in Deum* (giving oneself believingly over to God). This third one certainly includes the two preceding forms, yet in such a way that 'faith' implies, by its very essence, the response of the whole man." *Dare We Hope That All Men be Saved? With a Short Discourse on Hell* (San Francisco: Ignatius Press, 1988), 172-173.

De Lubac as well underlines the crucial significance of that third movement of the act of faith: "Here we have three acts which are linked to each other and follow a necessary progression. Only the third, which presupposes and incorporates the first two, characterizes true faith. *It alone makes one a Christian"* (emphasis added). *The Christian Faith: An Essay on the Structure of the Apostles' Creed*, trans. Richard Arnandez, F.S.C. (San Francisco: Ignatius Press, 1986), 141.

48. De Lubac, *The Splendor of the Church*, 33.

49. Joseph Ratzinger, *Introduction to Christianity* (New York: Crossroad), 55.

50. *"Amando, in eum tendere."* Commentary on the Sentences, III, d. 23, q. 2, a. 2, qc. 2 co.

51. De Lubac, *The Christian Faith*, 145-146.

52. "'This Church, constituted and organized as a society in the present world, subsists in [*subsistit in*] the Catholic Church, governed by the Successor of Peter and by the Bishops in communion with him.' With the expression *subsistit in*, the Second Vatican Council sought to harmonize two doctrinal statements: on the one hand, that the Church of Christ, despite the divisions which exist among Christians, continues to exist fully only in the Catholic Church, and on the other hand, that 'outside of her structure, many elements can be found of sanctification and truth' that is, in those Churches and ecclesial communities which are not yet in full communion with the Catholic Church. But with respect to these, it needs to be stated that 'they derive their efficacy from the very fullness of grace and truth entrusted to the Catholic Church.'" (Congregation for the Doctrine of the Faith, *Declaration "Dominus Iesus" on the Unicity and Salvific Universality of Jesus Christ and the Church*, August 6, 2000, 16.)

53. "When even a single act of sexual abuse by a priest or deacon is admitted or is established after an appropriate process in accord with canon law, the offending priest or deacon will be removed permanently from ecclesiastical ministry, not excluding dismissal from the clerical state, if the case so warrants" (Essential Norms for Diocesan/Eparchial Policies Dealing with Allegations of Sexual Abuse of Minors by Priests or Deacons, no. 8).

54. As explained on the USCCB website: "The United States Conference of Catholic Bishops established the National Review Board during their meeting in June of 2002. The functions of the Board were revised slightly and reconfirmed in June of 2005 when the *Charter for the Protection of Children and Young People* was revised and extended through 2010. The purpose of the National Review Board is to collaborate with the USCCB in preventing the sexual abuse of minors in the United States by persons in the service of the Church."

55. As one informed source pointed out to me, the Charter begins with an apology that was not present in the initial drafts, but was later inserted by the express wish of the bishops: "Since 2002, the Church in the United States has experienced a crisis without precedent in our times. The sexual abuse of children and young people by some deacons, priests, and bishops, and the ways in which these crimes and sins were addressed, have caused enormous pain, anger, and confusion. As bishops, we have acknowledged our mistakes and our roles in that suffering, and we apologize and take responsibility

again for too often failing victims and the Catholic people in the past. From the depths of our hearts, we bishops express great sorrow and profound regret for what the Catholic people have endured."

56. *Evangelical Catholicism*, 133.

57. According to a 2013 report by the Center for Applied Research in the Apostolate (CARA) commissioned by the U.S. Conference of Catholic Bishops, nearly a quarter (23 percent) of Catholics in the United States in 2012 reported that they had "no confidence" that the Catholic bishops as a whole were addressing the problem of sexual abuse of minors. Another 38 percent reported having "only a little confidence." That suggests that nearly two-thirds of American Catholics have little or no confidence that American bishops are responding adequately to the crisis. See Mark M. Gray, Carolyne Saunders, and Mary L. Gautier, *Catholic Awareness of Church Policies and Procedures to Deal with and Prevent Clergy Sex Abuse* (Washington, DC: Center for Applied Research in the Apostolate, 2013).

58. Homily to victims of priest sexual abuse, July 7, 2014.

59. Pope Francis, along with his nine cardinal advisers, had unanimously endorsed an initiative according to which a new judicial section within the Congregation for the Doctrine of the Faith would be established to handle cases of episcopal malfeasance in relation to the protection of minors from sexual abuse. Notwithstanding the papal go-ahead, the initiative became stuck in a quagmire.

60. In his apostolic letter *As a Loving Mother* (promulgated on June 4, 2016, and put into effect on September 5, 2016), Pope Francis offered some clarification as to the nature of the "grave reasons" for which a bishop (according to Canon 193.1 of the *Code of Canon Law*) could be removed from office. Among other forms of negligence or malfeasance, he specifically noted "the negligence of a Bishop in the exercise of his office ... in relation to cases of sexual abuse inflicted on minors and vulnerable adults." The letter goes on to specify that a bishop "can be legitimately removed from this office if he has through negligence committed or through omission facilitated acts that have caused grave harm to others, either to physical persons or to the community as a whole. The harm may be physical, moral, spiritual or through the use of patrimony," and "in the case of the abuse of minors and vulnerable adults, it is enough that the lack of diligence be grave." The letter then goes on to specify the canonical procedures under which evidence of malfeasance could be presented, and the case investigated and adjudicated.

61. The resignations of both Archbishop John Nienstedt of Minneapolis-St. Paul and Bishop Robert Finn of Kansas City-St. Joseph came in 2015. To date, Finn is the only U.S. bishop to be convicted for failure to report an accusation of child abuse. Finn failed to inform authorities after the discovery that one of his priests was in possession of hundreds of images of child pornography.

62. In a thorough review of eight plausible explanations of why U.S. bishops, prior to 2002 and the Dallas Charter, did not use recourse to the established

canonical processes for dealing with clerics who abuse children, Nicholas Cafardi notes that the reluctance hinged precisely on this conviction that their first response to the priest should be "pastoral" rather than "punitive." He then goes on to observe: "An immediate reaction to this response is, of course, what about the bishop's pastoral solicitude for the victim? Where does the victim fit into this canonical scenario? In what is perhaps a blind spot in the Code of Canon Law, especially given modern sensibilities to the great harm perpetrated by the sexual abuse of a child, solicitude for the victim is not mentioned in the penal process. In the penal equation, the pastoral solicitude of Canon 1341 is solely for the perpetrator. This unfortunate equation often meant that the bishop never even talked to a victim or the victim's family." (Nicholas Cafardi, *Before Dallas: The U.S. Bishops' Response to Clergy Sexual Abuse of Children*, 21.)

63. *Reconciliatio et Paenitentia*, 16, emphasis my own.

64. I thank my colleague Father Richard Veras for his observation that the Torah supposed that the sin of a Levitical priest brought guilt upon the whole people: "If it is the anointed priest who thus does wrong and thereby makes the people guilty, he shall offer to the Lord an unblemished bull of the herd as a purification offering for the wrong he committed" (Lv 4:3).

65. As a longtime sociologist and expert on the phenomenon once observed: "Clearly, complex psychological, cultural, and political processes are in-volved in recognizing and responding to childhood sexual abuse. Turning from the societal level to the individual level, the idea that individual experi-ence, psychological problems, or other psychological processes influence a person's willingness to entertain the possibility that many children are sexu-ally abused is consistent with current understanding in psychology about how individuals deal with anxiety-producing ideas or experiences. There is little doubt that the issue triggers anxiety. Recognition that children in gen-eral are at risk for sexual abuse, or that a specific child has been abused, is distressing for many adults because of their own histories as victims or vic-timizers; because of the affection adults feel for children; or because abuse involves emotionally-laden issues of relationships, sexuality, coercion, and other difficult intra- and interpersonal processes. Thus, because child sexual abuse stirs up strong emotions, denial, minimization, and rationalization have always played a central role in the societal response to child sexual abuse." Jon R. Conte, "Child Sexual Abuse: Awareness and Backlash," *The Fu-ture of Children* 4, no. 2 (1994), 227.

66. See Gray, Saunders, and Gautier, *Catholic Awareness*.

67. From a conference delivered by Msgr. Stephen Rossetti in Athlone, Ireland, to delegates to the first national conference on safeguarding children, February 28, 2015.

68. Ibid.

69. Ibid.

70. From an interview with Pope Francis by the official Jubilee publication *Credere* released December 2, 2015.

71. See also 2 Corinthians 6:11-12 and 7:15; Philippians 2:1-2; and Philemon 7, 12, and 20.

72. Peter S. Williamson, *Ephesians*, Catholic Commentary on Sacred Scripture (Grand Rapids, MI: Baker Academic, 2009), 123.

49042702R00117

Made in the USA
San Bernardino, CA
11 May 2017